PENGUIN BOOKS
**The Revolution
in Australian Politics**

Katharine West writes with wide experience in the field of Australian politics and public policy as a well-known broadcaster, lecturer, author and specialist consultant to government departments, major companies and community organisations. She was Senior Lecturer in Political Science at the Australian National University, Canberra, until 1979 and is now a Senior Associate in Political Science at the University of Melbourne.

D0806502

The Revolution in Australian Politics

KATHARINE WEST

Penguin Books

Penguin Books Australia Ltd,
487 Maroondah Highway, P.O. Box 257
Ringwood, Victoria, 3134, Australia
Penguin Books Ltd,
Harmondsworth, Middlesex, England
Penguin Books,
40 West 23rd Street, New York, N.Y. 10010, U.S.A.
Penguin Books Canada Ltd,
2801 John Street, Markham, Ontario, Canada
Penguin Books (N.Z.) Ltd,
182–190 Wairau Road, Auckland 10, New Zealand

First published by Penguin Books Australia,

Copyright © Katharine West, 1984

Typeset in Century Old Style and Helvetica by Dudley E. King, Melbourne

Made and printed in Australia by Dominion Press–Hedges & Bell

West, Katharine.
The revolution in Australian politics.

ISBN 0 14 007939 4.

1. Australian Labor Party. 2. Conservatism –
Australia. 3. Australia – Politics and government –
1976– . I. Title.

324.294'07

Acknowledgements

This book expands on some of the ideas I briefly outlined earlier this year in *The Bulletin* of 26 June and 3 July. I would like to thank the Editor-in-Chief, Trevor Kennedy, and the Editor, Trevor Sykes, for publishing these articles as a two-part series on 'The Hawke Revolution'.

Feedback from this series, and from the many radio and television commentaries I have given over the last two decades, is reflected in the underlying theme of this Penguin: that the most constructive discussion of national politics should focus on policy ideas and social values rather than on struggles for power, privilege and profit.

I would like to thank the Council of the University of Melbourne and my colleagues in the Political Science Department for the opportunity to write this book as a Senior Associate in Political Science.

I would also like to thank Penguin Books Australia for their commitment to the importance of promoting community debate on a wide range of complex national issues. In particular, I am grateful for the way in which Penguin's Publisher, Brian Johns, has viewed *The Revolution in Australian Politics* as a contribution to that debate, and has encouraged its writing and publication. No one could have been more imaginatively supportive nor more thoroughly professional in his editing than John Curtain.

Among my many debts, the deepest is to my parents, Sir Harold and Lady (Elizabeth) White. With their constant sense of community responsibility, they have always been among the most forthright and constructive of my critics. So too is my daughter and friend Caroline.

University of Melbourne
October 1984

1

The quietest revolutions are often the most dramatic. The quieter they are, the more easily they are entrenched without public recognition or debate.

So it is with the Hawke revolution, which has aspired to nationalise the Australian political system through its rhetoric of national unity and its strategy to capture the conservative as well as the middle electoral ground. /1

2

Life would be easier for self-styled consensus politicians if their political credibility were not being constantly challenged by those genuine and deep differences of opinion that exist in our community in the many areas that do not lend themselves to consensus decisions. /27

3

The real value of consensus politics is its potential to lock the whole Australian community into confronting our most pressing national problems. However, this potential has not yet been realised, in part because no effective pressure has been applied by the Opposition. /59

Contents

4

We are now moving into a new era in Australian politics when creative ideas and rational policy-making will matter more than ever before. For our major national problem is no longer merely the *political* one of how to redistribute community wealth. We also have the new *economic* problem of how to create wealth in the first place, while accommodating the need for greater security and stability in our changing social environment.

1

The quietest revolutions are often the most dramatic. The quieter they are, the more easily they are entrenched without public recognition or debate.

So it is with the Hawke revolution, which has aspired to nationalise the Australian political system through its rhetoric of national unity and its strategy to capture the conservative as well as the middle electoral ground.

In the name of consensus, the Hawke Government has been attempting a peaceful takeover of the Opposition in this country, and has been finding the task unexpectedly uncomplicated.

Too timid to be seen to be challenging the consensus ethos that had won the 1983 election for Labor, the Liberals failed to identify from the outset the policy areas where consensus does or should exist, and the areas where it does not or should not exist. This kind of early selective approach to consensus would have made it more difficult for the Hawke Government to attract the generalised support it has since received as a flow-on from the community's support for Labor's consensus stand on a specific issue: the need to replace conflict by co-operation in the area of industrial relations and wage fixation.

Lacking the required conceptual clarity and political courage, the Liberals got off to a very poor start after the 1983 election by offending one of the basic rules of effective politics: always try to avoid debating on your opponents' ground in your opponents' terms. Its initial refusal to buy into the consensus issue meant the Opposition condemned itself to precisely this fate. The Government was given the flying start from which the Prime Minister was able to consolidate his electoral image as a winner.

Effective opposition to the Hawke Government would have been more than a matter of refusing to accept its generalised consensus approach. It also involves understanding the political environment and the complex process of change within it. This is hard for a Liberal Party more attuned to retarding change than to promoting it. Yet this static perspective explains the Liberals' failure to adjust to the variety of ways in which the Hawke Government has been quite revolutionary.

There is more to the Hawke revolution than a so-called Labor Government deliberately setting out to capture the conservative vote with the rhetoric of conservatism – with the language of social order, the concept of community consensus, and patriotic appeals to national solidarity.

There is more to the Hawke revolution than the commitment of a so-called Labor Government to the traditional conservative goal of national economic growth – a commitment that has led the Hawke Ministry actually to deliver the conservative free-market economic policies the preceding non-Labor Ministry merely talked about.

As I forecast before the National Economic Summit last year[1] (when it was almost un-Australian to be heard saying such a thing), the most significant of the many aspects of the Hawke revolution would turn out to be its attempt to alter, in an ultra-conservative corporatist direction, the whole process of political democracy in this country. It was obvious that with its emphasis on the national unity structure of the Summit (later institutionalised in the Economic Planning Advisory Council, popularly known as EPAC), the Hawke style of government was going to focus on what I described then as the three major power blocs in Australian society: government, big business and unionised labour. This interpretation was taken up by Andrew Peacock as Leader of the Federal Opposition, and later by the media. It has now become one of the conventional perceptions of the Hawke Government.

Not surprisingly, some Labor supporters did not like my suggesting in March 1983 that the Prime Minister's glorification of the government-business-union triad evoked aspects of the classical theory of Fascism that lay behind Mussolini's Italian corporate state. There is, of course, a basic difference. The Hawke style of government has always involved skilfully-managed, co-operative consultation rather than coerced uniformity. But while the context of the two kinds of corporatism has been very different, the result has been the same in so far as in both Hawke's Australia and Mussolini's Italy the triad has been used to help lock the community as a whole into support for policies the Government desired.

The basic thrust of the Hawke corporate Government has been management and control rather than representation of the full range of community opinion. Labor's corporatism has been geared to achieving Government economic policy objectives – especially union co-operation in securing wage restraint – rather than to encouraging the free expression of conflicting and diverse views.

There is no doubt that the Hawke Government marks a distinct break with the pluralistic kind of pressure group politics to which we have long been accustomed in this country. Until recently, Australian politics had been essentially the push and pull of sectional interest groups which, regardless of their special relationship with particular political parties, were clearly separate from the Government they were trying to pressure. But with the advent of Labor's corporate state, as they were drawn first into the Summit and then into EPAC, business and union interests lost much of their capacity to act as independent operators.

For the business community as a whole – in contrast with individual business leaders accorded privileged opportunities to consult with Government – the sacrifice of institutional independence threatened the worst of both worlds. Because the full range of sometimes contradictory business interests was wrongly assumed to be reflected in the opinions expressed by the select group of businessmen attending the Summit and EPAC, the business community as a whole has been saddled with direct responsibility for a number of assertions and decisions it has not universally endorsed. (In this context, many will remember the controversy surrounding references to the taxation of capital gains made by chief executives Brian Kelman of CSR and Alan Coates of AMP.) Moreover, since it is easy falsely to claim that business interests have all had their say beforehand, they have been under considerable unspoken pressure to remain silent if they don't like the outcome of their nominal participation in political decision-making – or if they don't like the way in which at the Summit and EPAC business executives have tended to be overshadowed or out-manoeuvred by the growing union drive for greater power in the management decision-making process of companies as well as Labor Governments.

Up to a point, increased union power has been inevitable, since the Prime Minister has structured his whole Government around the existence of the Prices and Incomes Accord. Business, by contrast, has had no Accord. As Sir Arvi Parbo pointed out as Chairman of Alcoa and Western Mining and President of the influential Business Council of Australia:

MANY ENTERPRISES COMPETE with each other, and some businesses benefit from public policy measures which are a burden to others . . . It is therefore not possible for business to speak with one voice in all matters.[2]

Notwithstanding these internal conflicts, business has still had an important moderating influence within Labor's corporate state structures by emphasising the need for union wage restraint in a context of company profit recovery. What appears to be subordination to union interests is sometimes tactfully low-key effective dialogue between

'The basic thrust of the Hawke corporate Government has been management and control rather than representation of the full range of community opinion.'

senior business executives and union statesmen like Simon Crean and Bill Kelty.

This is not to deny that on occasions some companies and industry organisations – notably the Business Council of Australia and the Australian Chamber of Commerce – have expressed strong public reservations about proposed policy directions of the Hawke Labor Government. The size of the Budget deficit has been a constant source of concern to responsible business interests urging a much lower deficit than the Treasurer seemed at one stage to be contemplating. Business can play and has played a vital economic role in preventing the Prime Minister from being able to condition the community to accept what business believes should be totally unacceptable.

Indeed, the potential power of business over the Hawke

Government is far greater than Australians seem to realise. Since business co-operation and approval are essential to consolidating Labor's electorally desirable image as a 'responsible' administration, business interests have potentially much stronger bargaining power than they have so far exercised. For Labor has no alternative but to go to whatever lengths are necessary to prevent damaging business criticism of the kind that would attack the political credibility of the Government's consensus rhetoric. Business has never under any post-war Australian national government had the political clout it could now have under the Hawke Government if it chose to exert it. It may have to do so after the next election if, in the eyes of business, our Dr Jekyll Prime Minister threatens to reveal himself as Mr Hyde on the central issues of the size of the Budget deficit and the raising and spending of public funds.

At the moment, however, many company executives appear relatively relaxed about the performance of the Hawke Labor Government and its Treasurer, Paul Keating. Some might say they are naively relaxed, soothed by the flattering experience of easier and more direct personal access to the Hawke than to the Fraser Ministry. The crucial difference is often described in terms of closer co-operation and more effective consultation about specific company needs. But it is more than a matter of the different administrative styles of the two Governments. Policy substance is also involved. Many business executives believe they have been able or will be able to achieve company goals they could not achieve under the preceding non-Labor Government.

In other words, the fact that business criticism has been less hard-hitting against the Hawke than against the preceding Fraser Government may, in many cases, be less because of the restraining influence of the Summit and EPAC than because of a perceived coincidence of specific economic interest between individual companies and the Government. Indeed, one of the most dramatic aspects of the Hawke revolution is the close association with the current Labor Government of many major business interests which used to be exceptionally closely linked with the Liberal Party. An outstanding example of this metamorphosis is BHP, which in July 1984 publicised its impressive profit performance with what were widely regarded at the time as free advertisements for the Labor Party throughout the Australian press.

> **'Business has never under any post-war Australian national government had the political clout it could now have under the Hawke Government if it chose to exert it.'**

Under the banner heading WHAT INITIATIVE, HARD WORK AND CONSENSUS HAVE ACHIEVED, BHP endowed Labor's corporate state with the special legitimacy only business could provide. The endorsement could not have been more favourable to the Government had Bob Hawke written it himself:

WHEN INDUSTRY, UNIONS and Government got together a little over a year ago, the message was clear.

With consensus, hard work and bold initiatives, we could return this country to a healthy, stable condition, and keep it that way.

The healthy profit just announced by Australia's BHP is tangible proof of it.

A year ago, our vital steel industry was losing money at a rate which endangered its long term viability.

With Government co-operation where it was needed and justifiable, with constant constructive dialogue between BHP and Unions, and with BHP honouring its commitment by investing funds and increasing efficiency, the steel industry has made a very healthy turn around . . .[3]

BHP's reaction to the Labor Government is not unlike the reaction of a number of other large companies which stand to gain from specific Labor policies.

But even without a vested interest in specific Labor policies, many companies feel they share with the Hawke Government a primary concern for increased growth and a reduced rate of inflation. Until they see evidence that these general economic aims have been abandoned or are not being fulfilled, such companies seem prepared to give Labor if not positive support at least the benefit of any doubt. Moreover, Labor's corporate state – Australia Incorporated – is often praised in the business community as the best hope this country has of making the necessary structural and attitudinal changes to prevent further decline in our capacity to hold our own in increasingly fierce international economic competition. A variety of respected business leaders would doubtless have shared the cautious optimism of the chief executive of Westpac Banking Corporation, Bob White, who after seventeen months' experience of the Hawke Government publicly observed of Labor's relations with business: 'So far, it's all working'[4].

The comment was doubly significant coming from Westpac, formerly the Bank of New South Wales, which since 1945 had been not only, presumably, a major contributor to Liberal Party funds but also the most active of Australia's companies in promoting in the community the traditional Liberal free enterprise philosophy.

Obviously, the relatively amicable relations between the Hawke Government and much of Australian business reflect far more than shared participation in the Summit and EPAC. Far more too than the inevitable restraints on business criticism imposed by what in retrospect has been widely acknowledged as the major business error of endorsing a Summit communique that placed the necessary emphasis on a collaborative economic culture but too little emphasis on the need for a return to savings and profitability. The relatively smooth business-Government association also reflects economic factors external to the structures and processes of Labor's corporate state.

The basic fact is that many companies, like many unions, are generally happier with the Hawke than with the preceding Fraser style of economic management. The results of this management have been unambiguously better in Hawke's first term of office than in Fraser's last, and, despite Opposition claims to the contrary, these economically more favourable results can in part be credibly attributed to the practical benefits derived from Hawke's more conciliatory, compared with Fraser's more polarising, approach to politics and economic problems.

The negative impact of Malcolm Fraser's polarising style was the theme of the Alfred Deakin Lecture[5] I gave in September 1980, just before the Fraser Government almost lost a Federal election to the Labor Opposition led by Bill Hayden. After five years in government, the Fraser Liberals, I argued, were demonstrably out of touch with community opinion:

CERTAINLY RECENT PUBLIC opinion research suggests that many voters are coming to realise the self-destruction involved in our traditional dog-eat-dog sectional politics.

More and more Australians claim to be seeking national direction not from leaders acting sectionally – whether they be politicians, unionists or businessmen – but from all three of these groups acting together.

If this trend continues, the political popularity of leaders will in the future depend on the extent to which they can present themselves as competent mediators, balancing the competing interests within the policy-making triad of the three major organised power blocs in Australian society: big business, unionised labour and Government.

In this context, it is interesting to reflect on the favourable public response to the idea of ACTU President, Mr Hawke, as a potential Labor Prime Minister, following his systematic attempt to project precisely that kind of conciliatory image. An increasing number of Australians, it seems, are seeking not a party but a community leader, who will talk less about social divisions than about social consensus.

Two and a half years later, that precise scenario was fulfilled with the election of a Labor Government led by Bob Hawke.

While there continues to be strong community support for a less polarised style of politics than in the Fraser era, it is doubtful if voters are fully aware of many of the wider implications of the Hawke corporate state. For example, business participation in the Summit and EPAC has certainly undermined the national economic interest by diluting the strength of business protests against the limitations of the Prices and Incomes Accord in controlling the dominant element in the rising cost of employing Australian labour: the soaring non-wage labour costs involved in payroll tax, annual leave loadings, workers compensation and now the union drive for systematic superannuation schemes.[6] By contrast, the national economic interest has been promoted by the way in which union participation in the Summit and EPAC has diluted the strength of the more militant union pressures that have been so embarrassing for past Labor Ministries when exerted from outside rather than inside the Government's policy-making structures.

The Hawke Government has used national unity structures not only to deflect criticism but also to broaden the responsibility (or blame) for any of its unpopular decisions. Hence the Prime Minister's revolutionary claim in March 1983 that if there had to be some delay in giving the tax cuts he had promised before the election, it would not be because Bob

> 'The basic fact is that many companies, like many unions, are generally happier with the Hawke than with the preceding Fraser style of economic management.'

Hawke decided so. It would be because the community had decided so through its representative National Economic Summit. Not only was it extraordinary that in the context of tax cuts the Prime Minister chose to ignore the fiscal responsibility of Cabinet. Even more extraordinary was the way in which, in the process of broadening responsibility, he equated the Summit with the community.

Obviously it would be easier for a Government to manage and control a political community if the definition of that community could be narrowly confined to the corporatist triad of Government, big business and unionised labour. But in fact the representatives of this triad who attended the Summit could by no stretch of the imagination be considered adequately representative of the total social community.

Where among the voting delegates was *un*organised (as

opposed to unionised) labour? Where with more than observer status were the representatives of the (both registered and hidden) unemployed? There was only one representative of small (in contrast with big) business. Yet small business employs half the Australian work force. There were no voting delegates to represent the *former* work force – the pensioners. Nor was there any specific representation of the diverse group of Australian women – more than half the Australian population – united by a common concern to widen their capacity to exercise genuine freedom of choice: to rear young children at home, to participate effectively in the work force outside the home, or to do both consecutively. Where were the representatives of Australian consumers (as opposed to producers)? The list of the uninvited delegates could go on.

There is no question that in the old pluralistic kind of pressure group politics, the Australian political community was more synonymous with the social community and far wider than the big three organised power groups on which in 1983 the Summit was based.

When its membership was announced, many interest group leaders understandably voiced their protest at the way in which, under the Hawke concept of democracy, the effective political community had suddenly shrunk. This shrinkage left an obvious vacuum, which a well-coordinated Opposition could have very effectively filled. The non-Labor parties would have greatly improved their electoral credibility if they had set out systematically to raise the political consciousness of all the diverse groups excluded by the new Hawke corporatism, and likely to be disadvantaged by its decisions in the short or longer term.

This kind of systematic strategy was never implemented, partly because of the negatives typically found in opposition parties of inertia, shortage of the necessary intellectual input and factional rivalries reflecting different policy positions and conflicting leadership aspirations. Accentuating these handicaps was that special brand of cynicism politicians call electoral realism that drives them to calculate - no matter if they are in opposition or government - how far they can afford to champion the interests of one group without losing too many votes from another. The result is often conspicuous stalemate.

But the basic cause of the current Opposition's failure to implement a systematic strategy is its reluctance to think analytically about politics, instead of merely responding to the process

> **‘The Hawke Government has used national unity structures not only to deflect criticism but also to broaden the responsibility (or blame) for any of its unpopular decisions.’**

like players in a short-term sporting event. In striking contrast with their Labor counterparts, Liberal politicians are ill at ease with conceptual interpretations of Australian politics. Yet a coherent analysis of some of the more revolutionary aspects of the Hawke Government could have electorally embarrassed the Labor Ministry. If repeated often enough, an incisive critique of this revolutionary Government could have provided a credible framework and purpose for what has otherwise appeared a scatter-gun Opposition approach to issues.

The Opposition might have argued most effectively, for example, that despite the emphasis on consensus decision-making at the Summit and EPAC, the Hawke Government has promoted through these bodies a new kind of political class structure in Australian society. It has created a new kind of polarisation between the organised and politically powerful on the one hand and the unorganised and politically powerless on the other; a polarisation between the big three power blocs, Government, big business and unionised labour, and the rest of us in the Australian community.

'The rest of us' could have been vividly presented as the Opposition's natural constituency, comprising a clear majority of the electorate excluded from the political power structures of the Hawke corporate state.

With the Labor Government adopting an increasingly conservative approach to economic management, the Liberal and National Parties needed to re-define the contrast between Government and Opposition in terms of access to political power and influence: the minority in-group depicted as being promoted by the Government and the majority out-group represented by the Opposition.

Of course, more than rhetorical support was required from the Opposition. The varied and specific interests of the majority out-group had to be carefully identified and positively assisted in a wide range of constructive policies. Such policies would have directly challenged the credibility of Labor's traditional claim to be more deeply concerned than non-Labor about the oppressed in Australian society.

Rather than take advantage of this perfect opportunity to out-compete Labor on its own philosophical ground, Andrew Peacock chose instead to redefine Liberalism in his 1983 Alfred Deakin Lecture[7] very much in terms of the free-market conservatism that was already being pursued in the Labor Government's economic management. His approach was endorsed two months later in the Valder Report[8] on future directions for the Liberal Party.

This impersonal brand of economic conservatism lacked

the electoral appeal that a political out-group theme would have had. It also failed to provide any real contrast with what Labor was already *doing* in the economic area (unlike the Opposition Liberals who were confined to merely *preaching*). While the free-market emphasis did nothing for the Liberals' electoral support, at a critical time in July 1983 it shored up party support for Andrew Peacock as Federal Leader. It was exactly what the Liberal Party faithful and relevant influential business interests wanted to hear.

At the same time, this free-market conservatism was totally different from what marginal voters wanted to hear out there in the electorate. Party games have nothing to do with scoring electoral goals. Indeed, the two are often in irreconcilable conflict.

'But the basic cause of the current Opposition's failure to implement a systematic strategy is its reluctance to think analytically about politics, instead of merely responding to the process like players in a short-term sporting event.'

But a leader who fails to play the party game, or plays it poorly, runs the risk of being removed from the political field for good. So Andrew Peacock was careful to preach free-market orthodoxy in the Deakin Lecture where it didn't lose votes but won party applause.

On the hustings, however, his basic message was 'you've been robbed - or soon will be'. 'Dry' economic theory was replaced by the concrete concerns voters easily understand: the rising burden of taxes and charges, the threat to independent schools, and the attack on the right to a financially secure retirement. These were the simple themes which Andrew Peacock used in his successful by-election campaigns in the marginal electorates of Bruce in Victoria and Moreton in Queensland.

Had these specific themes been coherently linked to a broader attack on the consensus assumptions and minority power structures of Labor's corporate state, Andrew Peacock would have projected a distinct sense of political direction different from Labor. The obvious way to make the link was to emphasise that inherent in the birth of corporatism was the death of individualism in this country; inherent in the emphasis on the minority political in-group is the exclusion of the majority out-group. In other words, the Opposition should have argued that the new corporatism has given a contemporary relevance to the traditional Liberal emphasis on individualism.

Certainly, the new corporatism has given a new meaning to the philosophical clichés Liberal politicians have always mouthed about the importance of protecting and promoting the interests of the individual. For in the Hawke corporate state, individual interests are submerged by the dominance of the politically organized and economically powerful minority. Of course it is somewhat of a paradox that after three decades of rule by a Liberal Government professing to believe in the rights and interests of individuals, individualism should gain its most positive meaning in Australian politics as a negative reaction against the conservative structures and values of a corporate state promoted by a Labor Government philosophically committed to collectivism.

If it is valid to deduce political values from political rhetoric - a controversial assumption at any time - it would be fair to say that the Prime Minister thinks less in terms of individual people than in terms of what he calls 'the great interests' in this country: the Big-Three power grouping of Government, big business and unionised labour. It is relevant to reflect on how seldom the Prime Minister talks about *individual* Australians or select *groups* of Australians, other than business and unions.

Business and unions are a conservative, corporate-state variant of the traditional Marxist stereotypes of capital and labour. But in Bob Hawke's political world, the emphasis is on the possibility of co-operation between these two economic groups, whereas his 'Socialist Left' party colleagues stress the inevitability of conflict.

The traditional Liberal emphasis on individual autonomy is wholly absent from the Prime Minister's political scheme of things. Instead of talking about individual Australians, he couches his rhetoric in terms of all Australians or the Australian people or Australia's inter-

> ‘Business and unions are a conservative, corporate-state variant of the traditional Marxist stereotypes of capital and labour. But in Bob Hawke's political world, the emphasis is on the possibility of co-operation between these two economic groups, whereas his 'Socialist Left' party colleagues stress the inevitability of conflict.’

est. This emphasis on patriotic general categories is essentially conservative. It also conveniently obscures the gross economic, social as well as political inequalities that still exist under the Labor Government between some Australians and others. The Opposition might have found real political difficulty in championing the needs of the havenots at the expense of the perceived rights of the haves. But it would certainly have gained electorally by pointing out that the Prime Minister's preoccupation with general categories crowds out the essence of Liberalism, which depicts the *individual* as the basic political unit rather than the community as a whole or the groups with economic power. Bob Hawke is strongly conservative, but he is not a Liberal. Indeed, the Prime Minister's attitude to individualism is in the same mould as his attitude to the process of decision-making. Both attitudes are ultra-conservative, reflecting the perceptions and values of a corporate state leader.

But there is one aspect of his corporate state that is not conservative, and that is the Labor Party of which the Prime Minister is in theory the Leader. From the time he won the 1983 election, Bob Hawke was acutely aware of the need to promote something even more revolutionary than his corporatism. He had to distance his national Government that aspired to be conservative from his sectional party that many voters perceived to be radical. This distancing would have to be a continuing operation, adjusted to changes in the factional balance within Labor.

There is no doubt that it was easier for Bob Hawke to distance himself from his own party than it would have been for any of his predecessors in the Labor leadership. For he entered national politics despite the Labor Party, rather than because of it. He won his way into the Federal Parliament from an independent power base that was related only indirectly to the Labor Party as such – or even to the trade union movement. Admittedly, he skilfully used both of these sectional groups to gain his political objectives. But he used them to build up for himself the essentially non-sectional image of an agent of national reconciliation in divisive community disputes.

Paradoxically, it was this explicitly non-party image that made him a party leader, because enough of his parliamentary colleagues believed it was more popular with voters than the party image they perceived Bill Hayden as projecting. A number of these parliamentarians failed to recognize the extent to which Hayden's effective 1980 campaign had already broadened and strengthened Labor's impact across conventional party lines.

Hayden nearly won that election with his direct and persistent appeal to what used to be the electoral ballast of Australian Liberalism – the people I described in radio commentaries at the time as the downwardly-mobile genteel poor: conservative suburban families with dependent children and rising household costs. But

> 'There is no doubt that it was easier for Bob Hawke to distance himself from his own party than it would have been for any of his predecessors in the Labor leadership. For he entered national politics despite the Labor Party, rather than because of it.'

three years later, determined to gain office, Labor politicians were less concerned with gratitude for Bill Hayden's 1980 performance than with optimism about Bob Hawke's current personal popularity rating, which revealed widespread community support.

Then, as now, this rating depended on more than his superb camera presence and the magnetic empathy – that special kind of two-way trust – he has managed to establish with all generations of Australians. Bob Hawke's high ratings also seem to depend on his seeming to be outside and above party politics. The basis of his electoral value to the Labor Party and trade union movement depended on his not being seen to be linked exclusively or too closely with any of their more militant sectional interests. This need to preserve a non-sectional image has always given the Prime Minister both the incentive and the excuse for claiming the unprecedented degree of personal autonomy he has so far exerted as an Australian Labor Leader.

This autonomy, however, had to be vigorously defended when publicly challenged in the impassioned uranium debate preceding and during the ALP National Conference in July 1984. This debate threatened to destroy the essential electoral image of Bob Hawke as a man outside and above sectional Labor politics. The uranium controversy threatened to expose the Prime Minister's real Achilles heel: the fact that Labor Prime Ministers and Premiers are always in greater danger than their non-Labor counterparts of being dragged into internal party conflict because their leadership has been destabilised by factional disputes and personal rivalries.

In non-Labor politics, an electorally successful Leader can expect to be free of the destabilising impact of policy factionalism and threats to his own position from within his own party. Such rivalries are typically confined to non-Labor Leaders when they are in opposition or have failed in government to legitimise their leadership position through an acceptable level of electoral success. In non-Labor politics, overt factionalism most commonly occurs when a Leader has been soundly defeated in an election or has never had the opportunity to win one. Disruptive factionalism is invariably a sign that the Leader lacks the electoral legitimacy required to command respect and authority with party colleagues, with influential interest groups and with the community as a whole.

Labor politics are totally different. Factions are institution-alised regardless of a Leader's electoral success or failure. They are a permanent aspect of the normal functioning of the ALP in government as well as opposition. Overt factions are not a reflection of the Leader's relative lack of authority and electoral pull. They do not vanish or quieten down merely because a Labor Leader performs well at an election. On the contrary, in Labor politics overt faction-alism can actually increase following an exceptionally strong electoral endorse-ment of the Leader. This has been obvious in the Labor Party since Bob Hawke became Prime Minister.

> 'In non-Labor poli-tics, overt factional-ism most commonly occurs when a Leader has been soundly defeated in an election or has never had the oppor-tunity to win one.'

Despite the fact that he was given a clear personal mandate to govern, after his elec-toral victory a new Centre-Left faction was formed, effec-tively mobilised by the former Leader and current Minister for Foreign Affairs, Bill Hayden. In the short term at least, this faction has helped to stabilize rather than destabilize Bob Hawke's leadership authority. For in the course of the July party conference, faced with a choice between the arguments for conservative electoral pragmatism and more radical ideo-logical purity, the Centre-Left chose the former. But in the longer term, this powerful faction is obviously determined to ensure it receives adequate tradeoffs for its mobilisation of party support for the Prime Minister. If the Centre-Left is less successful than it would like to be in retaining its dispro-portionate representation in the Labor Cabinet, it will presumably compensate by increasing the open pressure on any re-elected Labor Government to do more than Labor has so far done to broaden the economic and social opportunities for the rapidly expanding ranks of the havenots in Australian society.

Despite any radical aspirations for the future, the Centre-Left has, to this point, played a crucial role in ensuring that the Prime Minister continues to appear to be firmly in control of the less conservative elements of his own Labor Party. There is no question that the Prime Minister's electoral position would have been severely weakened by any widespread perception that on key issues the policy stance of his Government was being dictated by the Socialist Left. As things turned out at the Conference, the decisive influence on voting outcomes was less the radical pressure from the minority Left than the relatively conservative reaction to this pressure from the Centre-Left. This moderating faction acted as the vital fulcrum of the Conference, modifying without destroying the conservative image Bob Hawke needed to project to Australian voters before the next national election.

Ironically, the consolidation of the Prime Minister's authority depended on the marathon performance before and during the Conference of the man Bob Hawke had been accused of single-mindedly manoeuvring to displace as Labor Leader. The votes of Bill Hayden's Centre-Left faction enabled the Labor Government to continue on its economically conservative path – at least for the short-term future.

The ex-Leader's mobilisation of votes at the Conference was the first public demonstration of another key aspect of the Hawke revolution: the introduction of a ruling duumvirate, involving a de facto sharing of manipulative power between Bob Hawke in the electorate and Bill Hayden in the party. This informal division of political territory between the two men might not have pleased the Prime Minister, but it reflected the political reality that in the party Bill Hayden could deliver the policy votes for Bob Hawke that Bob Hawke could not deliver for himself. Bill Hayden may have been the ex-Leader in name, but in practice his leadership ability remained. This de facto duumvirate proved extremely helpful to a Prime Minister trying to minimise the party base of his Government and to bury the conventional notion that political parties are the pivot and engine of Australian political life.

> ‘In Labor politics overt factionalism can actually increase following an exceptionally strong electoral endorsement of the Leader.’

At the time of the Conference, the alliance seemed in Bill Hayden's political interest as well as the Prime Minister's. But this coincidence of interest may not last beyond the next election. Circumstances could arise where the ex-Leader is no longer prepared to offer to the Right the tactical assistance that has proved so invaluable to the Prime Minister.

But whatever Bill Hayden's longer-term interest, Bob Hawke's political debt to him is already obvious. Even before Hayden's masterly Conference performance, the former Leader had been widely respected within caucus for the dignity with which he had endured and risen above the personal trauma of being pressured into resigning from the party leadership to make way for Bob Hawke[9]. In July of the following year, Bill Hayden again gave vital assistance to the man who had replaced him. Throughout the 1984 Conference, the Prime Minister's power base on the Right was acutely conscious of its dependence for floor majorities on Bill Hayden's delivery of the disciplined vote of the Centre-Left faction which held the balance of power. Had this vote been less effectively mobilised, Bob Hawke would have been made to look far less like the non-party patriot of the successful 1983 election and far more like the Labor Leader he has never wanted to become. Left-wing-dominated Conference decisions would have made it impossible for the Prime Minister to isolate his leadership image from Labor's factional disease. They would have drawn him publicly into the Labor politics he needed to keep private. He would have been burdened with the prospect of having to try to sell an apparently radical party in basically conservative marginal seats.

Once he began to look like a sectional Labor Prime Minister, Bob Hawke would have automatically lost his relative advantage over a party rival like Bill Hayden, whose power base in the new Centre-Left faction covered a wider policy spectrum than the Prime Minister's power base on the Right. Indeed, at the time the Conference was held, it was widely believed that Hayden would probably win against Hawke in any caucus leadership ballot held in circumstances where the Prime Minister had been dragged into sectional Labor politics, to the detriment of his national community image.

There is no doubt that within the electorate Bob Hawke's position would have been greatly weakened by any widespread perception that the national party conference was controlling him, rather than the reverse. Bill Hayden's assistance was essential if the Prime Minister was to manage the ALP Conference apparently, if not actually, on his own terms. In a country that has always preferred patriotism to party, the most electorally acceptable way for the Prime Minister to respond to party pressures at the Conference was to be seen to be responding to them in a national rather than a party context. He needed to appeal to the Conference as he had effectively appealed to the electorate: not as a sectional Labor politician but as a non-partisan patriot.

Of course on an issue like uranium mining, where there are demonstrably conflicting views both inside and outside his own party, it would have been disastrous if the Prime Minister had argued his case in the same kind of consensus rhetoric he had used in urging the electorate to exercise wage restraint. Instead, he needed to argue in terms of his overriding obligation to protect and promote his own perception of the wider community

‘Another key aspect of the Hawke revolution is the introduction of a ruling duumvirate, involving a de facto sharing of manipulative power between Bob Hawke in the electorate and Bill Hayden in the party.’

interest for which he was primarily responsible as national leader.

In appealing to the national conference as a Prime Minister rather than a Labor Leader, he was able to project the positive image of being *for* something – the national interest, as he argued for it – when he was in fact also *against* a substantial body of opinion in his own party and the broader community.

While the media were preoccupied with interpreting the Conference as a triumph for Hawke or for Hayden or for both, its deeper significance was overlooked. For whatever the contrived appearance of party unity, the uranium debate had dramatised the existence in Australian politics of divisive issues of principle that lend themselves less to consensus than to conflict.

Although it is reassuring to reflect on the many positive and optimistic aspects of the Hawke revolution, it is realistic to reflect as well on the major pressures in our community for a counter-revolution.

2

Life would be easier for self-styled consensus politicians if their political credibility were not being constantly challenged by those genuine and deep differences of opinion that exist in our community in the many areas that do not lend themselves to consensus decisions.

Areas as diverse as the mining and export of uranium; states' rights; the racial content of Australia's migrant intake; organised crime; US bases in Australia; affirmative action for women; taxation of assets and savings; the rights of the private sector in education and national health care; foreign control of the Australian economy; abortion; Aboriginal land rights; environmental conservation; and the challenge to traditional social structures and attitudes.

All of these areas involve controversy over values and perceived matters of principle or over rights and freedoms. Far from being peripheral in today's politics, these policy issues are of growing importance to Australian voters. They are quite different from strictly economic issues which are more easily negotiable and more compatible with a consensus Government image. Consensus politics assume either shared opinions or the capacity to compromise between different claims. Compromise most easily occurs when the political argument is really over funds rather than values. Sometimes issues of principle can be wholly or partly reduced to (or bought off with) money, as in Senator Ryan's August 1984

Education Policy Statement, but this is often not the case. For this reason, it is no longer appropriate to talk of the hip pocket nerve as the only major determinant of electoral outcomes in this country. From now on, an increasing proportion of electors will cast their first preference votes for what they genuinely perceive to be matters of principle rather than economic gain – although there will always be the many voters who like to rationalise an essentially greedy vote as a principled one.

When values are at the heart of a political conflict, consensus politicians run into serious difficulties. For consensus politics assume either the absence of conflict because of shared opinions or the capacity to resolve conflict through compromise between different views and claims. Consensus by compromise is not possible when diametrically opposed values are involved. It is obviously much easier to achieve when the political argument is really over funds.

Many Australians, including the Australian Democrats and the non-parliamentary Nuclear Disarmament Party, are irrevocably opposed to uranium mining. For them the argument is not, as it was within the 1984 ALP National Conference, over whether there should be more or less uranium mining – as if the argument were of the same order as whether there should be more or less government funding for non-government schools. For those who are unequivocally opposed to uranium mining, the issue is unbargainable and thus incompatible with any Government claim to consensus politics[10]. Voters who feel strongly about a basic issue of principle such as uranium mining are likely to regard any enforced compromise with contradictory attitudes as totally unacceptable. This kind of zero-sum perception precludes consensus in any true sense of the term. A Government may impose a decision on an issue of principle, but the Government's action will never be legitimate in the eyes of those voters who regard their principles as having been ignored or explicitly rejected. Indeed, the legacy of electoral resentment is greater if the Government claims a consensus which obviously does not exist.

This is the greatest danger the Hawke Government could have been made to face had the Opposition been brave enough from the outset to challenge the fashionable consensus myth. The Liberal and National Parties needed to raise the level of political debate to an open discussion of the many differences in our community – some of them reconcilable, some of them not. Andrew Peacock should not have hesitated to remind Bob Hawke that the art of conciliatory politics is to work towards reconciling as many community differences as possible, without antagonising people by pretending that the differences they think important do not exist.

> 'Consensus by compromise is not possible when diametrically opposed values are involved. It is obviously much easier to achieve when the political argument is really over funds.'

The Opposition also needed explicitly to reject the view which the Hawke Government wanted voters to accept: that conservatism is about free-market and other policies for promoting national economic growth, and not also about the values and rights of private enterprise and small property owners. An effective Opposition emphasis on the second of these two themes would have made it impossible for the Government to capture the conservative as well as the middle ground in Australian politics merely by publicising innovatory free-market economic policies and favourable indicators of national economic growth.

The Opposition also needed to emphasise the traditional conservative values of social cohesion (not present in contemporary Australia); of continuity with the past and stability into the future; of thrift and reward for effort; of self-help and family responsibility.

True, the Opposition constantly referred to the conservative social values of self-help and thrift in its prolonged attack on the Government's proposed assets test on pensions. But under Andrew Peacock's leadership, the Opposition was never prepared to champion systematically, without qualification or apology, many other aspects of social conservatism that would have helped to attract the suburban family vote. This was the electoral cost of having as non-Labor Opposition Leader a man who interpreted Liberalism less in the Menzies terms of 'family, home and hearth' than in terms of freedom of individual expression and tolerance of conflicting views.

Unlike his more conservative deputy, John Howard, Andrew Peacock reflected the influence within the post-Fraser Liberal Party of small l Liberals who typically argue that social policies should above all protect the freedom of individuals to 'do their own thing'. In taking this argument to its logical but many would say socially irresponsible conclusion, small l Liberals often end up arguing that on social issues their party should take no clear stand at all—except on the importance of every one being free to think and do what he or she likes. To pass any kind of moral judgement or promote any kind of social preference is perceived as conflicting with the primary emphasis that small l Liberals invariably like to place on freedom of individual expression.

This small l Liberal attitude to social issues is a political variant of what anthropologists call cultural relativism: the notion that any cultural pattern is as valid as any other, simply because it exists. This is not unlike the line of argument used for many years to justify the continued protection of some of the more notoriously inefficient Australian industries. Apart from the fact that policy stalemate is the frequent outcome of small l Liberal perspectives, they also prevent an electorally effective non-Labor appeal being made across conventional party lines to marginal voters holding conservative views on a whole range of social issues. These issues include the rising rates of drug addiction, household theft, public vandalism and violence; the apparent lack of adequate discipline in many government schools; and the alleged increase in what are often described as permissive or libertarian influences in the class room and the media.

Most important of all in electoral terms, the influence of small l Liberal policy perspectives encouraged the Liberal Party to abandon the social obligation it once acknowledged to protect and promote the stability and security of the married two-parent family as the preferred social unit for raising Australian children. Under small l Liberal influence, there was no convincing attempt to build on the electorally successful pro-family tradition of Menzies Liberalism. This was wrongly considered to be out-of-date because of the dramatic social change in the last two decades and the entry of many more women into the workforce outside the home. The Opposition made a basic political error in failing to promote not only the stable family unit but also – more specifically – the economic, social and educational needs of Australian children.

This should have been the basis of a determined drive to recapture from Labor those marginal voters that Gough Whitlam, Bill Hayden and Bob Hawke understood so well in the 1972, 1980 and 1983 elections; those small-property-owning 'peasant' conservatives rearing their children and tilling the soil on their quarter-acre blocks in suburban Sydney and Melbourne. They are the decisive influence in the vote at every Australian election, and for all Labor's talk about radical reform and democratic socialism, it can only win if its message strikes a chord with city families sharing the essentially rural values of peasant conservatism.

A basic reason for the growing polarisation within Liberal ranks is the frustration that many big l Liberals feel that their party's social policies are framed more to reflect the values of radical feminism and the opportunities for women in the workforce, and less the conventional emphasis on the stable family unit and on the family-based care of children. Although it is obviously both possible and necessary to accommodate all of these needs in a balanced and sensitive set of policies, the small l Liberal orientation of relevant Federal and Victorian policy-makers has prevented the Liberal Party from consolidating the strong support it once received in conservative marginal seats from its emphasis on the values of stable family life, regardless of whether both parents were working outside the home or not.

While the Labor Government has not been prepared to fill this electoral vacuum by expressing a preference for one kind of social unit or relationship among many others, the Hawke Government has nonetheless taken a more explicitly conservative stand than the Liberals on the need for family stability. Ironically, it was the Hawke Labor Government rather than the non-Labor Opposition which in 1984 launched a media campaign condemning the unacceptable social and economic costs of marriage breakdown and family disintegration. Partly in response to this initiative, and partly to placate the increasingly public disquiet among big l Liberals, Andrew

Peacock attacked the implied inconsistency between Labor's family stability campaign on the one hand and, on the other, its readiness to lower the status of legal marriage. In a reference to Federal Labor's proposal that taxpayers should fund the overseas travel of de facto as well as legally married partners of parliamentarians, Andrew Peacock promised to abolish 'Bob Hawke's escort agency'.[11]

There is no doubt that if the Opposition Leader had been a different kind of person – intellectually and temperamentally committed to a systematically conservative approach on all social issues – he would have found it much easier to challenge the consensus image of the Hawke Labor Government. He would have been able to launch a strong political attack on the socially divisive stands that the Hawke Government has taken in key community controversies like Asian immigration, aboriginal land rights, sex discrimination and abortion. It is not simply that on social issues big l Liberals can provide a conservative contrast with Labor that small l Liberals cannot provide. It is also the more fundamental point that on all kinds of issues – not only social – the most electorally effective opposition to consensus politics comes not from those who emphasise tolerance of different views, but from those who emphasise the superiority of one view not shared by the Government.

> ‘Most important of all in electoral terms, the influence of small l Liberal policy perspectives encouraged the Liberal Party to abandon the social obligation it once acknowledged to protect and promote the stability and security of the married two-parent family.’

The strategically logical – although not personally possible – way for Andrew Peacock to oppose the Hawke Government was from the outset to deny that in many key areas the alleged consensus exists at all and to proceed to take an unambiguously different stand on a whole range of extremely controversial issues.

This was the effective strategy of the doctors fighting Premier Wran in New South Wales in 1984 to uphold their own view of the proper role of the private sector under Medicare. It was also the eventually most successful strategy of the thousands of parents who met to protest in Sydney and Melbourne in 1983 about the implications of Senator Ryan's 'hit list' of independent schools, and the threat it presented to the funding and viability of other independent schools in a dual system of education.

Health care and education are among the most obvious policy areas where the emphasis should be on promoting difference and diversity as being vital to protecting the quality of services provided and the genuine freedom of choice in Australian society. The Opposition needed to stress the extent to which in the dual health care and education systems the socially productive co-existence of public and private sectors has been constantly threatened by pressures from socialist ideologues within the Labor movement who strongly believe in the superior value of single, universal, public systems. While this more extreme view was not reflected in the original thrust of the Hawke Government's health and education policies, they nonetheless encouraged a disruptive confrontation between the public and private sectors. Subsequent revisions in the implementation of health care and education policies removed the worst aspects of the confrontation and helped to defuse the electorally damaging criticism that while the Hawke Government in its first year of office had supported the private sector in some of its key economic policies, the reverse had applied in some of its key social policies. Certainly the early performance of the Hawke Government had given considerable credence to Opposition and community accusations that in the areas of health care and education, militant socialists within the Labor movement were bent on ensuring that, far from strengthening the private sector, the new Labor Government would strengthen the public sector in ways that also weakened the private.

The Government backtracking that later occurred reflected a clear recognition within the Cabinet of the depth of private sector support in the marginal seats that would decide the outcome of any early national election. The Prime Minister had an obvious electoral interest in consolidating the conservative Hawke revolution by vigorously denying that his Government was working towards universal away from dual education and health care systems. Nevertheless, it can be fairly argued that the Government continues to differ from the Opposition parties in its longer-term commitment to alter the balance within existing dual systems in favour of the public sector.

'The Opposition needed to stress the extent to which in the dual health care and education systems the socially productive co-existence of public and private sectors has been constantly threatened by pressures from socialist ideologues within the Labor movement who strongly believe in the superior value of single, universal, public systems.'

Health care and education are not the only policy areas that anti-socialist crusaders have tried to use to embarrass the Hawke Labor Government.

There have also been the very broad and electorally sensitive areas of Government revenue-raising and the level and direction of Government expenditure. As well as Opposition warnings about too high a Budget deficit and constant speculation about the extension of capital gains and indirect taxation and the longer-term introduction of a wealth tax and death duties, there was a prolonged Opposition attack on the pensioner assets test as originally proposed by the Hawke Government in 1983.

Although the Liberals were able to agree that championing a group like the pensioners had no negative side-effects in the electorate, the assets test issue still gave rise to a somewhat clumsy balancing-act within the party – where a far too well-publicised tug-of-war occurred between those who wanted to denounce the principle of an assets test and those who only wanted to reject the form it had taken in the proposed legislation. Eventually the Opposition launched a strong public campaign against both the principle and the form of the assets test. Too strong a campaign, it could be argued, to give maximum benefit to the Opposition as well as to the pensioners. For under sustained Opposition and community pressure, the proposed assets test legislation was substantially amended to constitute a correspondingly less favourable issue for the Liberal and National Parties at the next Federal election.

There is always a delicate path for an Opposition to tread between being seen to protest strongly enough against an unpopular Government proposal, but not to the point of forcing the kind of amendment that lets the Government off the electoral hook. The same point could be made about the Opposition's handling of Labor's original proposal to phase out Government grants to the richest non-Government schools. It is all too easy to spoil an otherwise effective political strategy by seeking what so many politicians seem to enjoy: the psychic thrills of overkill.

There was, of course, a logical challenge to consensus politics that the Opposition never made – although it was one of the most conceptually obvious and potentially one of the most effective challenges that could have been made. The Opposition needed to stress the absence in Australia of the required structural base for consensus politics. Such politics need a single coherent social, economic and political system through which consensus can be achieved and declared. Yet in Australia there is no such thing. Instead, there are two unequal societies, two contradictory economies, and two competing levels of government.

Instead of the one Australian society Bob Hawke keeps talking about, there are in fact two Australian societies: one for the millions of relatively affluent Australians and another for the growing number of those in poverty.

The gap between the two societies is constantly widening, and the ranks of the havenots are constantly swelling as more and more Australian parents and their children join the ranks of our most rapidly growing and most vulnerable group: the new poor. Victims of unemployment and/or family breakdown, the members of this group have no real place in Australian society, isolated as they are from the physical and emotional support structures they once enjoyed in the traditional middle or working class from which they came. Indeed, in combination, the downwardly-mobile new poor and the upwardly-mobile new rich have in effect replaced the old working class that used to form the solid core of Labor's electoral support. And the once stable middle class that used to form the solid core of Liberal support in the heyday of

Menzies Liberalism is now a quite different social amalgam, with new members having moved in from the ranks of the old working class and old members constantly moving out into the ranks of the new poor.

The relatively affluent in today's society – many of them in marginal seats – would prefer not to be told too much about the poor, especially if politicians want to suggest that the problem of poverty should be solved by income redistribution as well as economic growth. So the Government and Opposition have tended to leave it to the Australian Democrats and to socially responsible community leaders to draw attention to the depths of inequality in this allegedly egalitarian and lucky country.

Significantly, it was not a Government or Opposition politician but one of the two final contenders for the Anglican Archbishopric of Melbourne, the Executive Director of the Brotherhood of St Laurence, who called for a national war on poverty. In his Open Letter to the Prime Minister on behalf of Australia's poor, Canon Peter Hollingworth challenged, with a legitimacy only a respected church leader could possess, the whole credibility of the Prime Minister's consensus theology. As the public had so often heard, The Word, according to Bob Hawke, was that there was one Australia, united by a sense of optimism based on national economic recovery. The social reality, according to Canon Hollingworth, is that there are two Australias – one for the haves and another for the havenots.

This of course implies that consensus, where it applies at all, applies only to and for the haves. Canon Hollingworth's appeal to the Prime Minister for greater Government expenditure to help the poor could not have been made at a politically more awkward time for a Labor Government framing an election Budget aimed at attracting conservative marginal voters:

THERE HAS GOT to be an all-out, systematic, co-ordinated program to eliminate poverty. All our experience shows that it is never done in stops and starts. Most of all, it takes will-power – political will. You know all about personal willpower, and I firmly believe that you can marshal it politically. The eradication of poverty may well mean that the haves would have to make do without a continually rising standard of living for a time. That is politically tough, certainly, but if anyone can sell that to Australia, you can. There is nothing more certain, however, that if you don't, there will be no bringing Australia together, no real national reconciliation.

> 'Instead of the one Australian society Bob Hawke keeps talking about, there are in fact two Australian societies: one for the millions of relatively affluent Australians and another for the growing number of those in poverty.'

We will drift up to 1988, the beginning of our third century, as a nation deeply, harshly, and perhaps irrevocably divided into two Australias. That phrase should ring bells with you – as I recall, you were the first public figure to take Disraeli's famous words in the context of the widening gulf separating the affluent and the poor in Australia. We will have created through complacency, through a measure of greed and lack of compassion, another whole lost generation. It is slipping away from us, Bob, probably faster than we know, another whole cycle of poverty beginning to roll through Australian life, maiming and wasting all in its path. Is that the sort of Australia we want?

I can't think of a better place to start than in this year's Budget . . .[12]

In appealing to the Prime Minister to do something really significant to reduce the growing inequalities in this country, Canon Hollingworth discussed the poor not as a statistical abstraction but in terms of the human tragedy of family poverty and its destructive effects on the one in five Australian children – more than three-quarters of a million children – now forced to endure it. A rapidly increasing number of these impoverished children suffer not only financial disadvantage but also, as he stressed, the emotional trauma of parental unemployment, or family disintegration, or a crippling combination of both:

FAMILY POVERTY HAS taken root in Australia. You know that it has been talked about by social policy makers and welfare agencies for some years now, having taken over from the poverty of the aged as the focal issue. Family poverty means child poverty. The easiest path to poverty these days is to have a couple of kids, get retrenched, or separate from your spouse. It is almost inevitable. Just the other day, the Institute of Family Studies released some recent research which showed that up to 540,000 families had an income in 1981-82 less than the poverty line. This was an increase of more than 22 per cent since the ABS survey of 1978-79, and even more disturbing, the Institute said, was that among types of family below the poverty line, married couples with children had increased by more than 54 per cent and those in one-parent families had grown by more than 38 per cent.[13]

Another two horrifying statistical facts emphasise the depths of Australia's social crisis. First, the percentage of children under sixteen who are children of social service beneficiaries has more than quadrupled in the last decade, from 4.4 per cent in 1973 to 18.2 per cent in 1983. Second, about one in every seven households with dependent children is a single-parent household – double the level of the mid-'sixties.

The crisis of family poverty is one we are all facing in this country, the haves as well as the havenots. For the relatively affluent Australia will not be able to go on for very much longer pretending the other Australia, with its deep-seated poverty, does not exist. However much the haves may wish to deny it, many of the privileged and many of the underprivileged are emotionally linked in a common heritage, which means their futures are also inseparable. The black American writer James Baldwin expressed it well in a recent interview with a white American reporter. To adapt his remarks to Australia, read 'affluent' and 'poor Australians' for 'white' and 'black Americans':

THE TROUBLE WITH white Americans is that they do not know . . . that their history is inextricably linked with black Americans. The American dream? If it doesn't include me, it doesn't include you.[14]

But there is also a specific contemporary economic reason why family poverty should be the concern of the haves as well as the havenots. For the haves are expected to pay for the havenots, even though more and more of the taxpaying haves feel they are themselves falling into the ranks of the havenots as they struggle to rear their dependent children with inadequate income and inadequate family tax concessions. While strong reservations are now being widely expressed about the taxpayers' future capacity to fund adequate support for Australia's aged, what we should also be talking about is the immediate problem of their capacity to support Australia's young.

It used to be taken for granted that the rearing of children was the financial responsibility of their families. Nowadays, responsibility is more and more often being shifted on to the State – that is, to taxpayers required to fund not only their own children but other people's children and their lone and/or unemployed parents as well. It may seem callous to talk in such cash-register terms about the trauma of family breakdown and unemployment and the consequent emotional and financial poverty of children. But it is probably the most politically effective way the Opposition might have drawn attention to the problem. There will certainly be no community (and therefore no political) will for a drive against family breakdown and poverty until the haves are made to understand the limits of their own capacity to go on subsidising at an increasing rate other people's families as well as their own.

While Canon Hollingworth has a justified concern about the immediate need to relieve the hardship of Australia's poor, the longer-term solution to the growing poverty problem lies not in more Government money but in greater Government emphasis on social responsibility: on the responsibility of Government to ensure that socially useful work is always available for the otherwise unemployed, and on the responsibility of parents to look after their children's interests before their own when the two sets of interests conflict.

The promotion of a proper sense of family responsibility used to be central to the Liberal Party's philosophy and practice. It was one of the distinguishing features of the long Menzies reign, when the traditional liberal emphasis on individual freedom was adequately tempered by a counteracting conservative emphasis on social responsibility. Now, with its dominant small l Liberal commitment to the overriding freedom of adults to do 'whatever turns them on', the current Liberal Party has vacated the socially conservative pro-family territory the big l Menzies Liberals once firmly held. The vacuum has been filled not only by the National Party but also to some extent by the Australian Democrats, who have focused on the vulnerability of children as a key election issue.

If the Prime Minister wants to place his own Labor Party in socially conservative territory, to complement the Hawke Government's conservative economic revolution, he needs to confront the tragic growth of family poverty by stressing its attitudinal as well as its structural causes. If the Hawke Government is to give social credibility to its political rhetoric about a united Australia, it needs to acknowledge the extent to which the economic poverty of many of our children reflects the spiritual poverty of many of our socially irresponsible adults, as well as the lack of policy creativity among our politicians who have failed to cope with the problems of unemployment.

> 'While strong reservations are now being widely expressed about the taxpayers' future capacity to fund adequate support for Australia's aged, what we should also be talking about is the immediate problem of their capacity to support Australia's young.'

Not that the Treasurer, Paul Keating, dared raise such unpalatable truths in his optimistic pre-election Budget speech in August 1984. In the absence of a major restructuring of the taxation and welfare systems, the Budget strategy included no reference to the poor getting poorer and more numerous. There was no acknowledgement of the socially destabilising effects of the increasing polarisation between rich and poor in Australian society and the shrinkage of the middle class.

Statistics compiled by Phil Ruthven, Director of Ibis Corporate Services, have disturbing implications for the prospect of further confrontation and alienation in a community already divided between those with expanding, and those with declining, social and economic opportunities.[15]

On the one hand, Ruthven's statistics show that the relatively affluent (with incomes over $32,000 in 1981) have increased from 12.4 per cent of Australian households in 1969 to 20.2 per cent in 1981; and their share of total gross household income has risen from 25.1 per cent to 48 per cent over the same period. On the other hand, Ruthven's statistics show that the non-affluent (with incomes no higher than $22,000 in 1981) increased in number from 23.4 per cent to 29.5 per cent, and their share of total gross household income shrank from 9 per cent in 1969 to 8.5 per cent in 1981. Squeezed between these two extremes, the middle class (with incomes over $22,000 and under $32,000 in 1981) has declined from 64 per cent of all Australian households in 1969 to 50.2 per cent in 1981, and its share of total gross household income has crashed from 65.6 per cent to 43.6 per cent.

As was all too apparent in the reaction to the 1984 Budget, it is not possible to produce consensus politics merely by giving something more to everyone, without the Government also making a public commitment to a specific and coherent programme to reduce as quickly as possible the socially untenable gap it has inherited between those in real need, on the one hand, and two-income households with no dependent children on the other. Without the announcement of such a programme, consensus politics are incompatible with the glaring inequalities between our two Australian societies and with a Budget some of whose tax cuts for the haves have seemed as generous as some of the pension rises for the havenots.

Tax cuts for the haves may in fact be necessary to promote the opportunity for national economic growth. But unless they are accompanied by a concrete anti-poverty programme, they will merely accentuate the existing feelings of resentment and betrayal on the part of those for whom poverty threatens to be a long-term hardship rather than a temporary departure from a normal expectation of material comfort. The Government obviously needs to rely on more than the gradual trickle-down effects of national economic growth to raise the unacceptably low standard of living for the poor and many of the unemployed.

> 'If the Prime Minister wants to place his own Labor Party in socially conservative territory, to complement the Hawke Government's conservative economic revolution, he needs to confront the tragic growth of family poverty by stressing its attitudinal as well as its structural causes.'

No matter how dramatic the pace of our economic growth, it will never be fast enough in itself to defuse the potentially explosive effects of inequality in our community. The provision of a steady but minor increase in jobs for the otherwise unemployed will reduce the number of havenots, but it will do nothing to alter the relative poverty of those who remain in their ranks. Government strategies other than economic growth are also required. It is very small comfort indeed if politicians tell the havenots that some of them – the Government doesn't know whom – will at some time in the future have a chance of entering the ranks of the haves.

While the poor are waiting to see if they will be among the lucky ones, their hardship has to be relieved. Apart from anything else, many of the poor are lone parents who at least in the short term would be reluctant to enter the work force – whatever their training and whatever the state of the labour market – if they feel a direct personal responsibility to rear their dependent young children at home. It is an obvious over-simplification to depict the havenots as a cyclical aberration destined to join the ranks of the haves when the economy picks up. However humane it may seem to those who try to reassure the poor that they in fact have a future, unrealistic hopes often lead to disappointment and consequent alienation which, in extreme circumstances, could drive the poor to reject the political system itself as being totally inadequate for expressing and satisfying their overlooked interests and needs. If the current alienation of the havenots is allowed to reach this political extreme, Australia will risk the destructive instability that has characterised in so many parts of the world what sociologists have called the plural society.[16]

In this kind of society, the individual derives a sense of political community not from common citizenship of the state, but rather from membership of a particular social group within it. If Australia were allowed to develop into a plural society horizontally divided along the lines of the haves and the havenots, demonstrated sympathy for the havenots would be the only basis of all judgements made by the poor about the legitimacy of their political leaders. In those circumstances, winning government according to the constitutional rules of the game would not in itself make the victors politically legitimate in the eyes of the poor. Political legitimacy would be judged only in terms of whether or not the policy priorities of political leaders reflected an adequate understanding of the plight of the poor, and an urgent commitment to do something more positive about it than the simplistic and ineffective Robin Hood approach of trying to make the poor richer by making the rich poorer.

> ‘No matter how dramatic the pace of our economic growth, it will never be fast enough in itself to defuse the potentially explosive effects of inequality in our community.’

Every political community has to contend with competing interests, but there is a fundamental difference between the sorts of competing interests that merely endanger administrations and the sorts of divisions that in a plural society threaten the political system as a whole.

It is the difference between conflicts which occur within a basic political consensus and conflicts which, when taken to extremes, deny its existence. In a plural society, political conflict cannot be dealt with as it has so far been dealt with in Australia by fifty-one per cent (or thereabouts) democracy. For fifty-one per cent democracy implies an environment in which the interests that social groups have in common and wish their Government to promote are more important than the interests which divide them. It also assumes the existence of enough cross-cutting political divisions between social groups for the political majority to be a shifting, rather than the same, aggregate of interests on different political issues.

To avoid the development of a plural society in Australia, it is vital for politicians to convince the poor that they will be assured of a more and more reasonable minimum for themselves and that the relatively affluent will receive from Government funds no more than a reasonable maximum. The danger is that unless there is dramatic national economic growth, the minimums and maximums demanded by the two groups will in no way coincide. If the national economic pie to be distributed is seen to be not growing but constant or even diminishing, politics are more easily perceived as a zero-sum game in which one group's gain must automatically be another group's loss. This perception may not accord with the objective reality, but it nonetheless gives rise to extreme feelings of hostility, jealousy and despair.

The structural base for consensus politics involves far more than impressive national economic growth to help eliminate the glaring inequalities between people. It also involves eliminating inequalities between different economies within the same political unit. It is not surprising that past Governments have found difficulty managing the economy, since Australia doesn't have one for them to manage.

The Hawke Government, aided by its intellectually creative Minister for Industry and Commerce, John Button, has been the first Australian Government to acknowledge this in its attempts to talk coherently about our basic economic problem: that instead of one efficiently cohesive national economy, Australia has a number of economies. Two of them are quite contradictory, with one endangering the future of the other. The more efficient of these two contradictory economies is export-oriented, more internationally competitive and less protected than the other economy, which is inward-looking and internationally uncompetitive within a protected domestic cocoon.

The economy geared to international competitiveness is the key to Australia's future growth prospects based on mineral, rural, manufacturing and service exports. To the extent that it is able to be efficient by international standards, this export-oriented economy offers Australians the lucrative prospect of sharing in the dramatic growth projected for the adjoining West Pacific Basin. This is the region that the Rand and Hudson Institutes have forecast will have twice the potential of the world as a whole for growth in real GDP to the end of the

'The economy geared to international competitiveness is the key to Australia's future growth prospects based on mineral, rural, manufacturing and service exports.'

century. As a nation, Australia can either equip itself to participate in the enormous benefits of this regional growth or allow itself to be left out in the economic and political cold. There should be little doubt which choice the average voter would make if it was properly presented in those terms.

But because politicians have been reluctant to put the alternatives in quite so stark a form, most Australians have lacked any sense of urgency. Until their recent experience of an economic recession unparalleled since the Great Depression, Australians had been soothed by a cargo-cult mentality irresponsibly promoted by the Fraser Government's short-term electoral interest in fighting the 1980 campaign on the basis of extravagant resources boom rhetoric. Perhaps the Government actually believed its rhetoric. I certainly didn't, and shortly before the campaign began queried in my 1980 Alfred Deakin Lecture whether the projected growth would automatically occur:

THERE IS A significant gap between opportunity and achievement, although the fragility of development proposals is something our cargo-cult political leaders would prefer to ignore. Doubts don't win elections.[17]

Obviously Malcolm Fraser's boom rhetoric should have been challenged at the time by the mining companies, whose longer-term position was bound to be adversely affected by the inflationary wage claims fanned by the Government's undue optimism. But except for strong reservations stressed by the Australian Industries Development Association (AIDA), business chose to remain silent, upholding what in 1980 was still the very short-sighted business tradition of failing to communicate to Australians its problem of fragility as well as its prospect of strength. The mining industry soon learned its mistake, as overnight there developed a widespread image in the community of a cargo of mineral riches waiting to be distributed at once to all Australians. Instead of promising to come down from the skies, Pacific-Islands-style, Australian cargo was supposed to have already come out of the ground, having somehow miraculously by-passed the usual problems of lead-in times and cost-competitiveness to be sold at record prices.

These boom delusions were fast followed by an unambiguous economic bust, and by much economic soul-searching. For the first time since the end of the post-war reconstruction period, Australians have been ready to admit that if they want cargo, praying to the gods – even the right ones – is just not enough. They have yet to agree, however, on the need to develop a more coherent, outward-looking and competitive economy.

Indeed, there is some controversy about the likely response to any systematic attempt by the Hawke Government to project an economic 'light on the hill' involving the interdependence of Australia's future with something foreign. One school of thought argues that Australians will never respond enthusiastically to an outward-looking economic nationalism, since they are xenophobes to the core, disliking all foreigners, even those who speak the Australian language.

> ‘For the first time since the end of the post-war reconstruction period, Australians have been ready to admit that if they want cargo, praying to the gods – even the right ones – is just not enough. They have yet to agree, however, on the need to develop a more coherent, outward-looking and competitive economy.’

Another school of thought argues that because so many Australians are racists, the best way to encourage them to support a more outward-looking economic strategy is to warn them that if they don't support it, they are in great danger of becoming quite literally the poor white trash of their Asian region.

Certainly, until now, Australians have argued far less than they should about the way in which our export-oriented economy is undermined by the contradictory economy based on highly protected manufacturing. This economy offers no viable base for preventing Australia from falling behind not only other OECD countries but also other countries in the West Pacific region. The unnatural profits from this uncompetitive protected economy are the outcome of Government subsidies for the few, at the expense of greater long-term economic security for the majority. Cocooned protected industries are far removed from the reality with which export-oriented industries live precariously day by day: that economic growth in the contemporary world is not an assured birthright, but an internationally competitive race whose prizes are distributed on the very clear criteria of comparative cost and perceived reliability of supply.

Australians have been slow to understand the realities of this new economic world partly because, until the early 1980s, supporters of the protected economy had the political numbers or at least the most persuasive political voice. This was not surprising, given the way in which the Federal Parliamentary Liberal Party had long been dominated by the protectionist state of Victoria from which all national Liberal Leaders but one, Sir William McMahon, had come. The longserving national Leader of the Country Party, Sir John McEwen, was also a Victorian and a strong supporter of protected industry in the Coalition Government which Sir Robert Menzies led for almost two decades until 1966.

For the whole of the post-war period, the Liberals had in practice been irresponsibly casual about the irrational distribution of resources in the Australian economy.

Despite the increasingly obvious need for urgent action, successive non-Labor Governments were content to behave like the American satirist, Mort Sahl's, definition of a modern conservative. A conservative, he said, is some one who believes that nothing should be done for the first time, while a modern conservative is some one who believes that it should be, but not now.

In the mould of true modern conservatives, the non-Labor parties continued to engage in illogical double-talk aimed at securing the best of both political worlds by supporting both long-term structural adjustment and short-term excessive protection. The two were incompatible, in so far as the profits of heavily protected industry were sometimes so high that, far from contracting, investment was encouraged to expand. In this policy area, as in so many others, non-Labor Governments' concern for short-term political success seriously undermined the country's prospects for longer-term economic success.

By the end of Malcolm Fraser's period in office, the political clout of protected Victorian industry was being strongly challenged by other states and other economic interests which were increasing their relative power within the country and the coalition, at Victoria's expense.

> ❛In the mould of true modern conservatives, the non-Labor parties continued to engage in illogical double-talk aimed at securing the best of both political worlds by supporting both long-term structural adjustment and short-term excessive protection.❜

It took a change of government, however, before the political initiative was taken to improve the use of national economic resources by bold plans to rationalise first the steel and then the car industry. John Button's car plan was an interesting conservative variation on more conventional concepts of Labor planning. While the Government set the general parameters for the proposed rationalisation, the free market was left to perform the politically embarrassing task of deciding which of the existing companies might stand to lose from those parameters. The plan was not only rational economics; it also seemed to be very sound politics.

Notwithstanding Labor's major initiatives to improve the structure of two key industries, the fact is we still have no coherent economy. Australia still has two unequal and conflicting economies: one of them relatively efficient, unprotected and internationally competitive; the other relatively inefficient, protected and uncompetitive. Each Australian state varies in the extent to which it is propelled or retarded by the specific balance within its boundaries between these two quite different economies, one of which retards the competitiveness of the other. Indeed, as I have stressed in a recent discussion of federalism and resources development[18], in our federal system of government the potentially explosive inequalities are based less on the dichotomy between labour and capital than on the varying degrees of efficiency with which capital is used in different state economies.

Australian federalism is increasingly the politics of competitive economic regionalism, reflecting the uneven rates of economic growth in different parts of Australia. This means that the Hawke Government's commitment to national economic growth will be judged not only in terms of what it promises to deliver to the country as a whole but also in terms of what it delivers to voters in a particular state. Superimposed on the politics of individual inequality are the politics of state inequality. They inevitably exert an irrational and retarding pressure against the most rational Government strategies for maximising national economic growth.

Given these state inequalities and the absence of a coherently integrated single national economy, there is no automatic national economic interest – other than the economic consensus decreed by the Hawke Government as representing the kind of balance it is prepared to promote between protected and less protected economic activity. The need to govern in consensus terms does have the very positive advantage of forcing the Hawke Government to take a clear public position on key industry policy issues which preceding non-Labor Governments were able and anxious to evade. But the economic consensus declared by Labor politicians still has no appropriate structural base, given the continued existence of powerful but conflicting economies within the same political unit.

The absence of a structural base for economic consensus also explains the absence of a structural base for political consensus. For the existence of the two contradictory economies ensures unequal productivity in different states, which in turn prevents the opportunity for a single political system to form a coherent base for genuinely consensus politics. Instead, unequal productivity in different states has led to competitive regionalism and to the Balkanization of the Australian political system. Despite the Hawke Government's rhetorical emphasis on national unity and solidarity, the politics of the next decade will increasingly involve the assertion of regional economic rights and needs and differences.

Competitive regionalism affects not only the unity of the nation, but also the unity of its governing Labor Party. For apart from the impossibility of reaching a natural consensus

> **'Australia still has two unequal and conflicting economies: one of them relatively efficient, unprotected and internationally competitive; the other relatively inefficient, protected and uncompetitive.'**

among Left, Centre-Left and Right factions in the Labor Party, the assertion of regional rights and needs will inevitably cause serious conflicts of interest between different state branches and between national and state levels of government. This will certainly occur in 1985 if the Hawke Government faces budgetary difficulties requiring it to restrain state government expenditure.

But conflicts of interest within the Labor Party between the different state branches and levels of government will also occur on issues other than funds if Bob Hawke continues in office to assert his need to remain as far as possible a non-party Prime Minister. In such circumstances, even if there were a greatly strengthened non-Labor movement, the greatest political conflicts would be likely to occur less between government and opposition in the national parliament than between state and national Labor Governments. There are many who agree with the Prime Minister's own assessment that the greatest threat to him has always been not the formal opposition in the Liberal and National Parties but the informal opposition in his own ALP.

So long as the Hawke Government has sufficient largesse to distribute, many of the potentially divisive issues within the ALP are essentially bargainable – like the continuing controversy over redistribution of income and over the desirable balance to be struck in the Government's economic strategy between what the Prime Minister has termed equity and efficiency. Even issues of principle can often be reduced, at least in part, to money – like the rights of independent schools within a dual system of education.

But when money is short, the Government is certain to confront intensified internal party conflict between factions and states and levels of government. Which is why national economic growth is not only good for Australia; it is vital to the Prime Minister's own political survival, as both national and party leader. While an emphasis on national economic growth has traditionally been associated with conservative Governments, it is more important to the political security of a Labor Government. For if redistributive demands for greater equity cannot be met from the profits of economic growth, Labor politics must rapidly degenerate into a public dog-fight between ideological purists who want to extract heavy taxes from the haves, and electoral pragmatists who want to extract their votes. Beyond a certain point, these two desires are not easily compatible.

> *While an emphasis on national economic growth has traditionally been associated with conservative Governments, it is more important to the political security of a Labor Government.*

In the absence of an acceptable rate of national economic growth, Bob Hawke could well deal with his political quandary by swamping the left of his party through opening Labor's ranks to 'all Australians'. Imagine the success of a recruiting appeal projected in these terms by our most extraordinary ordinary Australian: an appeal directly reminiscent of the winning 'men and women of Australia' that opened Gough Whitlam's brilliant 1972 campaign.

But it would be misleading to see Bob Hawke's political future merely in terms of whether he can deliver economic growth or swamp the left wing of his party. This would suggest that all he has to worry about is handling the internal Labor Party conflict over financial values. But the Labor Party is a microcosm of the wider Australian community, in so far as both are increasingly concerned about the non-financial values that are central to the controversy over uranium mining and over a whole range of complex social issues.

Life in the Australian Labor Party and in the Australian community as a whole would certainly be closer to Bob Hawke's consensus ideal if we could all be persuaded actually to believe the myths and legends we have about ourselves: that we are an egalitarian country, free of glaring inequalities; a materialist country, unconcerned with social and moral values. If those myths and legends were true, any conflict that did occur would be limited in nature and easily amenable – like a money transaction – to bargaining and compromise. Any divisions could be easily healed by a skilfully-administered dose of Dr Jekyll's instant consensus medicine.

But Australian life is not like our myths and legends. We are not an egalitarian country. The polarisation between rich and poor is increasing, and the ranks of the long-term poor are swelling with people of all ages. This is one of a number of reasons for a growing number of Australians becoming deeply concerned about social and moral, as well as financial, values. The more the social fabric is seen to be disintegrating around us, the more urgent will be the community demand and the electoral need for our politicians to take a sensitive and positive lead by treating not the symptoms of our accelerating national problems but their basic causes.

3

The real value of consensus politics is its potential to lock the whole Australian community into confronting our most pressing national problems. However, this potential has not yet been realised, in part because no effective pressure has been applied by the Opposition.

If the non-Labor parties were serious about wanting to regain office, they needed to recognise that a self-styled national unity Government implies a national unity Opposition. If the non-Labor parties were to reveal the policy limitations of the Hawke Government, they had to project an alternative view of the national interest that was both more coherent and more forward-looking than Government perceptions. In other words, the Opposition parties needed to prove themselves a better set of patriots than their political opponents. They had to think nationally – not sectionally, as they have tended to do since losing office.

Admittedly, there was obvious electoral advantage in bundling together a rag-bag of disaffected sectional interests affecting the vote in marginal seats. But this scatter-gun approach accentuated the impression of an Opposition lacking any broad policy vision or any clear sense of national direction. This image would not have mattered so much if Bob Hawke had been behaving like a sectional party politician. But instead he was trying to appear the non-partisan patriot. His studied non-sectionalism clearly distinguished him from his explicitly sectional Liberal predecessor, Malcolm Fraser.

The Opposition seemed unaware of the basic difference between these two national leaders, and continued to live in the political past, reacting like a sectional party Opposition confronting a sectional party Government. The approach was jarringly out of tune with the current political mood and with the Prime Minister's determined drive to end party government by leading above party politics and across conventional party lines. In contrast with Bob Hawke's assertions of concern for 'Australia's interest', as he put it – wider and loftier than any limited party interest – the Opposition's sectionalism appeared carping and petty. It was also intellectually uncreative.

Had the non-Labor parties been more obviously interested in new ideas, the Hawke Government could have been easily challenged. For in fundamental ways, it has been conspicuously out of date, struggling to solve yesterday's problems, rather than tomorrow's. Admittedly this is not entirely the Hawke Government's fault, given the pile the Fraser Government had put aside into its politically too-hard basket. But the fact remains, the Opposition missed a perfect political opportunity to force the Hawke Government to lead a public debate about the basic problem any Australian Government must face: how to maximise national economic efficiency and competitiveness in a way that promotes adequate opportunity for all Australians, rather than some.

Of course, tomorrow's major problems are especially embarrassing to a Government seeking early re-election. For they inevitably demand a major restructuring of Australia's taxation, welfare, employment and industry policies: the kind of policy revolution the Hawke Government would not have wanted to flag unless obliged to do so by an insistent Opposition. Better from Bob Hawke's point of view to face the electors as Dr Jekyll and let Mr Hyde emerge later – if he must.

The Opposition, by contrast, had every electoral reason to assert that Mr Hyde had already emerged, but as a kindlier man before the poll than he would turn out to be after it. The original education, health care and pensioner assets-test proposals could have been depicted as indicative of the draconian actions that would be taken in other policy areas when, after the early election, the revolutionary Labor leopard changed its conservative blue spots back to radical red. This was potentially the most electorally effective scenario for the Opposition parties. But they destroyed its credibility by overkill criticism, which encouraged Mr Hyde to revert as quickly as possible to Dr Jekyll and substantially revise the most unpopular aspects of the Government's policies in three electorally vital areas.

If soon after losing office the Opposition parties had been able and prepared to construct innovative policy packages themselves, they could have deplored the unenterprising performance of the Hawke Government on key policy matters. For tomorrow's problems remain unsolved and in many cases unacknowledged. True, there has been debate about the future burden of pension payments to the elderly retired. But there has been no attempt to confront the implications of the ill-publicised fact that during the last decade, over two-thirds of the increased expenditure on welfare pensions and benefits have been directed to people of workforce age. Nor has there been any serious discussion about moderating the upward pressure on labour costs by more explicitly relating tax and welfare policies to genuine need.

If these and other problems are to be adequately solved, a revolution is required in our policy-making approach in this country. If the Hawke Government is to promote the national interest in practice as well as rhetoric, our inappropriately segmented style of policy-making needs to be replaced by a more comprehensive approach that recognises the interdependence of policy areas wrongly regarded as separate. Unless welfare, taxation, industry, wages and employment policies are considered in combination – rather than in isolation from one another – any Government will inevitably find it almost impossible to introduce the most socially as well as economically productive use of Australia's human and economic resources.

For it is not easy to take something away from marginal voters unless it is done as part of a wider policy package in which, with its other hand, the Government seems to be giving something back. The Hawke Ministry failed to adopt this politically advisable approach in its original proposal for an assets test on pensions. Instead, it defeated its desired policy purpose by addressing the problem with yesterday's piecemeal methods. Obviously both economic rationality and social justice required the whole area of retirement income to be considered in terms of a far wider concept of social security than the one the Government actually used: a wider concept embracing not only welfare but taxation and employment policies as well.

Segmented policy-making is a major defect in any Government professing a concern for greater equity. In the case of the Hawke Government, it left a disturbing policy vacuum which the Opposition parties needed to fill. But they lacked the intellectual capacity and commitment to rise to the occasion. For innovative policy formulation requires not only imaginative politicians but also something the present Liberals most obviously lack: a party tradition that values and promotes intellectual creativity and spirited policy debate.

In the Labor Party, both of these occur as the automatic

outcome of institutionalised and competitive factions. Those aspiring to ministerial office stake their claims to caucus election by indicating their preferred positions on a range of important policy issues. But quite apart from the policy emphasis in Labor factions and in the caucus selection of Ministers, there are always creative tensions built into any party committed to change and reform.

A concern for change and reform, however, should not be confined to Labor politics. In an era of acute national problems, any party aspiring to govern needs to be thinking in terms of major policy innovations. The trouble with the Liberal Party is it has no thinking mechanisms built into its structures and operating procedures. Quite the reverse. In the Liberal Party, policy disputes are too widely and too often viewed as a form of subversion, allegedly threatening to undermine party unity, or the Leader's position, or both.

> ‘It is not easy to take something away from marginal voters unless it is done as part of a wider policy package in which, with its other hand, the Government seems to be giving something back.’

This mattered less in the Menzies era when politics involved presiding over automatic economic growth rather than having skilfully to create and manage it. Now the environment is totally different. At a time when imaginative policy ideas are essential to cope with our social and economic problems, it matters a great deal when the Liberal Party tries to stifle, rather than nurture, the intense kind of policy debate which is central to the normal functioning of the ALP. Despite the traditional Liberal rhetoric about the importance of freedom of expression of conflicting views, there is no attempt to ensure this rhetoric is reflected in Liberal Party practice. On the contrary, all the pressures in Liberal politics are towards narrowing rather than widening the options and perspectives involved in the discussion of national policy.

But the Liberal Party's basic policy-making problem goes beyond inappropriate party attitudes. Even more it relates to inadequate party personnel. With notable exceptions in both parliamentary and organisational wings, the Liberal Party throughout Australia has been inundated with too many mindless careerists, hoping to use this political organisation to give them a rapid escalator ride to a public prominence they could not otherwise achieve by applying their limited skills in private professional and business life. Liberal politics has proved the quickest possible form of professional or social mobility for a large number of party members whose natural talents have been minimal.

Given the systematic way in which too many mediocre people have used the Liberal Party for personal rather than policy promotion, it is not surprising that the Liberals are out of government in every mainland state and at the national level. For we are now very clearly in a new political era in which the capacity and willingness to think are minimum requirements for an Opposition to regain office. The essence of successful electoral politics for an Opposition party today is the creation of something new: an alternative and intellectually more convincing vision of the national or state interest than that implied in Government policies. Alternatives like this involve the politics of ideas.

While creative thought is now a prerequisite for success in the electorate, it has traditionally threatened the prospects for personal advancement within the Liberal Party itself. For what typically wins inside the Liberal Party is not the capacity to develop new perspectives, but the skill to exploit the perspectives that already exist. The most relevant qualities for any one aspiring to do well in the Liberal Party are the qualities associated with the least innovative kind of business entrepreneur, who expands his or her power and influence by taking over something that has already been created, instead of creating something additional and new.

The people who succeed in the Liberal Party, but far less at today's polls, are not the builders of new frameworks but the manipulators of the old. These manipulators are skilled at protecting vested interests and the status quo, but obviously inept at delivering an opposition party's basic requirement of a *change* in the status quo. If the Liberal Party genuinely wanted to understand why it has performed so well at some national and state elections and so poorly at others, it should isolate as one of the key variables the balance in different campaign strategies between the advice of uncreative manipulators on the one hand and creative policy builders on the other. For the primary commitment of the manipulators is to their own power base in the party rather than to their party's power base in the electorate. This affects not only the quality of the party's campaign strategy and policies, but even

> ❛The most relevant qualities for any one aspiring to do well in the Liberal Party are the qualities associated with the least innovative kind of business entrepreneur, who expands his or her power and influence by taking over something that has already been created, instead of creating something additional and new.❜

more negatively the quality of the party's candidates.

The answer does not lie in more centralised preselection procedures if the values of ambitious branch members are merely replaced by the values of ambitious executive or administrative committee or policy assembly members at the centre. Whatever the stated intentions to the contrary, central intervention in Liberal preselections has too often involved a primary commitment not to the choice of quality candidates but rather to the development of personal political machines to use as the basis of bids for greater power in the party. In such circumstances, central intervention has involved careerist tradeoffs of mutual self-interest, regardless of the calibre of the candidates involved.

Those within the Victorian Liberal Party who supported the Elliott Report reforms aimed at securing greater policy input and preselection influence from the centre were unduly naive if they believed changed structures would in themselves secure an electorally better outcome from the party's point of view. The opinion polls in August 1984 were showing the State Liberal Party with even lower public support than at the time of Labor's sweeping state election victory in April 1982.

Unless there is a determined effort to protect and promote intellectual quality in a party, it will not surface of its own accord. Preselection is inevitably dominated by the values and interests of those who know how to manipulate the party machine. Their motivations are often in stark contrast with those creative policy developers, who would spurn the more blatant kinds of misrepresentation that too often accompany the preselection process in Liberal politics.

There are, of course, exceptions to this depressing picture of the people thrown up by what might euphemistically be called the 'dynamics' of Liberal politics. One of these exceptions helps to explain why, despite its major strategic errors in the last NSW state campaign, the Liberal Party has had markedly more electoral support in New South Wales than in Victoria. For the NSW Liberal Leader, Nick Greiner, has a policy builder's mind with the training and inclination to conceptualise political issues in a way the Victorian Liberal Leader, Jeff Kennett, has not been able to do. Because Greiner's intellectual competence is recognised by the electorate, he has been able to avoid the vicious circle that occurs elsewhere in Liberal politics, where an electorally unpopular party is further weakened by the

> 'Unless there is a determined effort to protect and promote intellectual quality in a party, it will not surface of its own accord.'

Leader feeling the need to surround himself with machine manipulators, who have the techniques to protect his leadership position within the party, but not the ideas required for the policy innovations that would promote his party's position in the electorate.

This lack of policy creativity is not confined to specific Liberal Leaders. It is typical of the overwhelming majority of Liberal politicians, strong on negative party rhetoric but weak on constructive policy argument. While the Opposition parties were very vocal about the need to meet the challenge of the recent economic depression in this country, they have been very silent about the need to meet the challenge of that other depression far more relevant to their immediate political fortunes: the intellectual depression within their own ranks.

In the national parliament, there are only a handful of

Opposition members able to match Labor's intellectually much sharper front bench. Except for the policy and debating contributions of a small minority of the shadow ministry, the only effective criticisms of the Hawke Government's consensus claims have come from individuals of varied political persuasions from outside the structures of party and parliament.

People like Canon Peter Hollingworth, who as Executive Director of the Brotherhood of St Laurence has daily confronted the realities of family poverty in that other Australia the Prime Minister seldom talks about. Or John Stone, who before retiring as Secretary of the Treasury felt an obligation unambiguously to express his strong reservations about the longer-term impact on Australia's economic future of the borrowing, protection and labour market policies being currently pursued under the Hawke Government. Or Geoffrey Blainey, Professor of History at the University of Melbourne, who insisted on his right in a democratic country to advance the opinion that the only viable immigration policy is one which avoids social hostility between those coming to Australia and those already here. Or the Nobel Prize-winning novelist Patrick White who reminded the Hawke Government that there are many thinking Australians who do not accept the moral validity of a decision to support the continued mining and export of uranium.

Many other reservations about the Hawke Government could be cited from respected people in business, the professions, the trade unions and community welfare groups. Their combined impact has called into question the credibility of the Hawke Government's consensus claims far more than the combined criticism of non-Labor parliamentarians. This explains the widespread view in the Australian community that any reasoned and constructive opposition in national politics has had relatively little to do with the Liberal and National Parties, which have failed to win what in many areas could have been an easily winnable debate if the Opposition had had the conceptual wit to fight on its own ground, rather than the Government's.

In choosing their own ground and sticking to it, Peter Hollingworth, John Stone, Geoffrey Blainey and Patrick White were far more sophisticated politicians than the non-Labor parliamentary opposition. Together with the Australian Democrats inside the Parliament, these four critics outside the parliament and others like them provided the Hawke Government with its only serious political competition by directly and effectively challenging its consensus claims on key policy issues.

‘In choosing their own ground and sticking to it, Peter Hollingworth, John Stone, Geoffrey Blainey and Patrick White were far more sophisticated politicians than the non-Labor parliamentary opposition.’

The relatively unimpressive performance of the non-Labor members has encouraged the old anti-intellectual jibes against the Labor Party to be redirected to the other side of parliament.

It has become increasingly obvious that one of the most significant aspects of the Hawke revolution is the concentration of an unusual degree of talent on the Government's front bench compared with its relative absence from the front bench of the Opposition. Although it is commonly regarded as intellectually arrogant and therefore un-Australian to draw such a distinction, it goes a very long way towards explaining why the Hawke Government has had such an easy political run. Many Labor Ministers have shown an impressive capacity for conceptual clarity in their discussion of policy issues. This is first and foremost what increasingly well informed marginal voters respect in their politicians. While some marginal voters may not agree with the context of the Hawke Ministry's message on certain issues, most of them would admire the way in which the message is usually conveyed. Labor has a real political edge over the non-Labor Opposition in an electorate where more and more voters want to hear logical and concrete explanations from their politicians, rather than stylised and meaningless polemics.

This seems to apply not only to the majority of voters in marginal seats, but also to the plain-speaking realists who predominate among Australian women, if not among Australian men. As I have often observed when asked about the changing political influence of Australian women, a rapidly increasing number of them are showing a highly informed interest in public policy, applying their finely-tuned 'crap' detectors to what politicians say. In this changing scene, more and more voters are looking for parliamentarians of human warmth and intellectual depth, with something concrete to say about urgent national problems. If the Liberal and National Parties had more such people in their parliamentary ranks, they would provide far stiffer competition for the Hawke Government than they have so far done. Marginal voters want politicians with more ideas than they have themselves about how to confront issues of genuine concern.

Straight and clear answers to complex questions will win votes. Rhetorical verbiage and evasion will lose them. Yet short of saying nothing, there is often no alternative to rhetoric if a party lacks a concrete policy to talk about.

This has been a central problem for the Opposition since

the Hawke Government came to power. For instead of seizing the policy initiative himself at the same time as he assumed the Opposition leadership, Andrew Peacock allowed the delegation to his deputy, John Howard, of the chairmanship of what turned out to be an unduly long policy-formulation process. Because it took so long for even the first of the Opposition's policies to be released, Andrew Peacock could offer no constructive policy alternatives during the crucial first year of his leadership. Yet it was vital to his own and his party's political future to challenge the Hawke Government's consensus claims with a contrasting Opposition view of the national interest.

> **Straight and clear answers to complex questions will win votes. Rhetorical verbiage and evasion will lose them. Yet short of saying nothing, there is often no alternative to rhetoric if a party lacks a concrete policy to talk about.**

Of course, it is an oversimplification to suggest that Andrew Peacock easily could have seized the policy initiative if he had wanted to lay down clear policy guidelines himself, instead of allowing them to evolve from a process controlled by his deputy. In non-Labor politics, policy coherence can be imposed from above only by Leaders with the authority to do so. In the Liberal Party, this authority can only be derived from a perceived capacity to win elections.

If a non-Labor Leader has not won the last election and is not given at least a fifty-fifty chance of winning the next one, he inevitably faces serious difficulties in imposing any concrete policy position at all. The problem of limited personal policy authority is compounded if, like Andrew Peacock, the Leader interprets Liberalism as demanding freedom of individual expression and tolerance of conflicting views. Policy coherence can never be achieved if the Leader is unwilling to override the potentially damaging polarisation between the small and big l Liberals. This polarisation was allowed to develop in the policy vacuum caused by the absence of Opposition policies for more than a year.

A number of Liberals of diverse policy views took advantage of this vacuum to try to improve their relative positions within the Opposition ranks. On the so-called left of the Liberal Party were the experienced Steele Hall, former Premier of South Australia, and from Victoria Ian Macphee, responsible for the controversial areas of employment and industrial relations and the status of women. On the so-called right of the Liberal Party were the shadow minister for immigration and ethnic affairs from Tasmania, Michael Hodgman (who never forgot to remind Australians that in his view this was the Hawke 'socialist' Government) and the no-holds-barred Wilson Tuckey from Western Australia. Politically effective battles were fought on the education issue by Peter Baume from New South Wales and against the pensions assets test by Tony Messner from South Australia. As Opposition Leader in the Senate, Fred Chaney from Western Australia made a constructive contribution to internal party discussion and to the projection of Liberal arguments on the media. Like David Connolly and Jim Carlton from New South Wales, he was aware of the need for new ideas in Liberal policy-making.

Other Liberals worked hard to try to promote their prospects within the party, but none worked as hard or as effectively as John Howard from New South Wales. Defeated by Andrew Peacock in his bid for the party leadership first time round, John Howard wanted to be better placed next time round in any leadership contest after the next election. His wide-ranging contributions to parliamentary debates showed a disciplined conceptual clarity, and in parliamentary tactics, more often than their colleagues, he and his senior adviser Michael Baume were able to pinpoint the relevant questions to ask the Government.

But the problem with John Howard was the same as the problem with Andrew Peacock. Both men tended to oppose the Government on its own policy ground, rather than stressing its limitations and calling instead for a revolution in the whole way in which we approach national policy issues.

> ‘In non-Labor politics, policy coherence can be imposed from above only by Leaders with the authority to do so. In the Liberal Party, this authority can only be derived from a perceived capacity to win elections.’

In considering the future prospects of Australian non-Labor politics and parties, there is an obvious need to distinguish between potential leaders who are skilled at fighting on existing ground and those with the creative imagination to redefine the ground at a higher level, with greater benefit to the general community interest and more positive appeal to marginal voters.

Certainly the Opposition parties could have opposed the Hawke Government much more strongly and systematically than they did for its failure to give enough attention to widening the opportunities for the havenots through an essential combination of economic growth, and new patterns and concepts of work. The Opposition should have explained to

Australian voters what the Government did not find it electorally convenient to admit: that without new patterns and concepts of work, a drive to maximise national economic growth will not in itself automatically widen social and economic opportunities for all – as opposed to some – Australians. At least in the short term, such a drive could narrow these opportunities.

For assuming the recent steel and automotive industry decisions are indicative of the general direction the Hawke Government wants to take, its broad economic strategies are aimed at increasing national wealth and international competitiveness through a more economically efficient allocation of Australia's resources, even at the cost of job shedding in affected industries.

The Opposition needed to spell out more clearly than it did the context of the Government's growth claims and the implications of future growth having to depend on the harsh realities of international competition. These implications were expediently buried by the Hawke Labor Government, which could not afford to admit the negative effects on international competitiveness of unduly high wage on-costs and the new drive for greater union control over the management decisions of companies and Labor Governments. Free from such constraints on their intellectual honesty, the Opposition parties should have emphasised the dramatic contrast between the old and new forms of post-war economic growth. They should have drawn the fundamental distinction between, on the one hand, the steady unilinear pattern of the cocooned kind of growth based on protected manufacturing – the growth of the Menzies/McEwen era of the 'fifties and early 'sixties – and, on the other hand, the corrugated ups-and-downs of the kind of cyclical growth based on the balance between supply and demand in a highly volatile and increasingly competitive international environment.

The Opposition could have discussed the way in which the Hawke Government has obscured the changing nature and meaning of growth by using the same term, 'growth', to refer to economic circumstances with social implications quite different from the past growth to which Australians have been accustomed.

In the Menzies/McEwen era, despite the importance of the export economy, there was heavy political emphasis on labour-intensive manufacturing for an insulated domestic market expanding through natural population increase and migration. Because the returns from protected manufacturing were both rapidly and relatively evenly distributed in a context of relatively low unemployment, the growth of the Menzies/McEwen era achieved a more general social legitimacy than the new kind of growth, which involves a far more uneven impact on different geographical areas and different groups of people.

'In considering the future prospects of Australian non-Labor politics and parties, there is an obvious need to distinguish between potential leaders who are skilled at fighting on existing ground and those with the creative imagination to redefine the ground at a higher level, with greater benefit to the general community interest and more positive appeal to marginal voters.'

The experience of the 'fifties and early 'sixties led the community to expect that economic growth would always involve immediate returns and a continuously rising standard of living for all but a few Australians, regardless of the factors of productivity and competitiveness that are vital to growth nowadays. There was no time-lag – no credibility gap – between Government references to growth and a perceived feedback into the average Australian hip-pocket.

Growth of the future is likely to be a quite different proposition. Returns from any capital-intensive resources development will not automatically be either rapidly or evenly distributed throughout the Australian community. Some economic activities and some state economies will benefit more than others, and in certain circumstances at the expense of others. While the community expects capital-intensive growth of the future to produce greater wealth than the labour-intensive protected manufacturing of an earlier growth era, in the short term at least any returns from resources development will be far smaller. For unlike growth based on protected manufacturing, resources development involves a long time span between the massive commitment of funds and the actual production of export income.

Yet community expectations telescope these two distinct stages of financial investment and financial return, arousing strong feelings of cheated expectations. Because Australians have no clear concept of the different time frames involved in the different kinds of post-war economic growth, there occurs across the whole economy the potentially crippling effects of what I have often referred to as the 'pre-emptive strike'. This is meant to convey not the idea of disrupted production, but rather the concept frequently applied to the imperatives of military strategy in the Middle East.

By the pre-emptive strike, I mean the determination of each Australian to stake his (or her) claim first for the biggest possible cut of the national economic cake, regardless of the cost to the economy or the community as a whole. Each

Australian tries to get in first for his cut – and as big a cut as possible – because if he doesn't, he perceives that somebody else will do exactly the same thing at his expense. The pre-emptive strike was at its worst in 1981 following the resources boom rhetoric of the 1980 Federal election campaign. The ensuing wage spiral was halted by the Fraser Government's essential wages pause. This was in turn consolidated by the Hawke Government's attempt to restrain direct wages (although not on-costs) through the Prices and Incomes Accord, ratified by the ACTU (although not by the Opposition parties or the business community). But with a marked rise in company profits in 1984, there has been a renewed threat of excessive labour costs arising from the union thrust not for higher wages but for a wider range of workers' benefits which the employer is being asked to fund.

The Opposition needed to challenge the credibility of the Hawke Government's growth claims by a spirited campaign against the debilitating effects of increasing labour costs on those potential growth industries whose whole future depends on being able to compete on international markets. Instead of concentrating its industrial relations argument on how wages should be fixed, the Opposition needed to hammer home the basic message that the cost of employing labour is in fact going up under the Prices and Incomes Accord and it is pricing more and more of our businesses out of international markets and thus more and more Australians out of jobs.

The Hawke Government would like the Accord to be perceived as a restraining influence, and so it may have been, together with the realities of a depressed economy. But the relevant question is not how present labour cost increases compare with those in 1981 but how present labour cost increases compare with those of our trading partners. There is no denying that under the influence of the Accord, labour costs have been institutionalised in excess of our inflation rate, which in turn is well in excess of the inflation rates of our main trading partners.

Labour cost increases are in excess of CPI increases because, in addition to virtually automatic indexation (which ensures the CPI increases due to exchange rate devaluation are quickly fed back into increased wage rates), there are provisions for so-called anomalies adjustments, the introduction of shorter working hours, a campaign under the label of 'occupational health and safety' (but covering far more than that), and a concerted drive to extend superannuation coverage (which unions themselves estimate will add three per cent to labour costs).

Arguments that superannuation can be funded from productivity increases overlook the extent to which productivity increases have already been consumed in ajustments following anomalies hearings, as well as the extent to which productivity increases result from capital investment and labour shedding. As the then President of the Business Council of Australia, Sir Arvi Parbo, perceived it:

The capital has to be serviced from productivity gains; thus not all can be available for additional benefits to labour. In the case of gains from labour shedding, made to keep the enterprises viable, it seems immoral as well as economically irrational to then distribute the gains in additional benefits to those still employed.[19]

Of course, the most constructive approach to rising labour costs is less to condemn them than to try to understand their basic causes. More is involved than the career interests and political ambitions of militant union leaders. There is also the failure of successive Australian Governments to recognise the impetus given to higher wage (and on-cost) demands by the limitations of our tax and welfare policies in acknowledging the needs of families with dependent children. Their relative shortage of disposable income has given a legitimacy to their claims for the higher wages which have fed through, without widespread community protest, to the workforce as a whole.

If these across-the-board, ever-increasing wage claims are to be restrained, policy makers need to ensure that wages, taxes and welfare are treated as interdependent and are considered together for their combined effect on employees' capacity to support their families. If policy makers are to prevent the upward push on labour costs, they need to acknowledge the way in which everyone's higher wage claims are tolerated in our society on the ground that many employees definitely require higher disposable income to rear dependent children in a society where social welfare is inadequately related to the tax structure and to family responsibilities.

> 'There is also the failure of successive Australian Governments to recognise the impetus given to higher wage (and on-cost) demands by the limitations of our tax and welfare policies in acknowledging the needs of families with dependent children.'

The Opposition failed to make the obvious political point that if the Hawke Government had been really serious about restraining labour costs, it would have talked less about the Accord and more about the need to ensure that social security and justice are achieved in this country through the appropriate welfare and tax policies, to enable the wage system to be unambiguously based on genuine productivity. The Opposition should have approached the spiralling labour cost problem by advocating the introduction of a more comprehensive concept of social security that linked the policy triad of taxation, wages and welfare.

Unless this triad is the conceptual basis of decisions made about the way Governments raise and spend public money in Australia, there will be no hope at all of the equity and efficiency Bob Hawke describes as his primary political goals. But to maximise social justice and economic growth, far more is required than the rejection of irrationally segmented thinking and the adoption of an adequately integrated approach to taxation, welfare and wages policy.

A revolution is also needed in the way politicians present their economic arguments to the Australian electorate. A polarising attack on protected manufacturing or special pleading for export interests obviously produces less widespread community sympathy for the requirements of international competitiveness than a consensus call for neutrality in the treatment of all economic activities. The drive for international competitiveness needs to be presented as an integral part of legitimate community concern for equity and efficiency in the management of all aspects of Australian economic life. Such a plea for even-handedness should get a good hearing in a society which talks a lot about the virtue of giving everyone a fair go.

Of course, the most economically efficient and equitable allocation of resources is not the most socially efficient and equitable allocation in the eyes of those who lose their jobs through industry rationalisation or the removal of Government subsidies. This kind of contradiction explains why a succession of non-Labor Governments has failed to make decisions about Australian industry in the best interests of the Australian community as a whole. The challenge for the Hawke Labor Government and all future Governments is to confront rather than bury the problem by adopting constructive strategies to overcome any negative social implications of the positive economic policies required to maximise national wealth.

There are a number of possible strategies. The least viable strategy is the one being adopted at the moment, of continuing to pay the dole to an such a very large number of unemployed. This is an economically unproductive and socially disruptive option that no Opposition should allow any Government to pursue. Apart from the waste of human resources and the personal suffering involved, the payment of the dole inevitably saps the economic vitality of the community as a whole. A welfare state mentality rapidly infects not only those receiving Government assistance but also those on wages. This lowers the economic productivity of the total society and produces the vicious circle where because less wealth is created, less money is available to help more people in need.

> ‘The Opposition should have approached the spiralling labour cost problem by advocating the introduction of a more comprehensive concept of social security that linked the policy triad of taxation, wages and welfare.’

In a capitalist or mixed economy, it is vital to retain the nexus between payment and productivity and to avoid giving something for nothing. It is all too easy for recipients of a so-called ‘social wage’ to come to regard it as a right, rather than something they should earn. Whether we are talking of a 'social' wage or an 'industrial' wage, neither should be paid to physically fit people of work-force age, except in return for some economically or socially productive work. Otherwise, there is justifiable resentment against those who are paid for doing nothing on the part of those who are paid for doing work, often work they do not particularly enjoy.

But the overwhelming social problem lies less in the justified resentment of the employed than in the feelings of worthlessness and rejection experienced by many of the unemployed in a society with such a glaring gap between its work ethic rhetoric on the one hand and its unemployment reality on the other. There is an increasing polarisation in Australian society between those who can and those who cannot define their own worth in terms of paid employment. The result is an alienated out-group of unemployed, for whom the dominant work ethic values of our society are at best irrelevant and at worst anathema. The Minister for Science and Technology, Barry Jones, expressed the sadness of it all:

For those who feel that loss of employment is a form of social death, the compulsory work ethic is a torment, forcing them in search of jobs that no longer exist and re-enforcing a prevailing conviction that to be unemployed is to be worthless.[20]

This unemployment creates a most threatening position for the haves as well as the havenots, as Australian society becomes more deeply divided and unstable. If maximum wealth is to be available to help to avoid a growing polarisation in this country, more is involved than a major adjustment to our wage, tax and welfare policies. The necessary combination of maximum economic growth and at least minimum social justice requires the early introduction of extremely innovatory employment policies. It is no longer acceptable to focus on a wages policy for the employed, without reference to an employment policy for the unemployed. It is not enough to respond, as the Hawke Government has done, by saying that growth will in itself create jobs. This is true, but the trickle-down effect works too slowly to cope with the acceleration of alienation and resentment among the havenots. The problem is compounded by the fact that the most effective forms of wealth creation often involve job shedding, and a changed emphasis on capital-intensive rather than labour-intensive production.

> 'It is no longer acceptable to focus on a wages policy for the employed, without reference to an employment policy for the unemployed.'

If the Hawke Government is serious about wishing to maximise both social justice and economic growth, it needs to preserve the work ethic, with its focus on productivity and reward for effort. But it needs to expand the relevance of this ethic to the community as a whole by encouraging it to apply to socially as well as economically productive employment.

The Government should no longer pay the dole as negative compensation for failure to get work. Instead it needs to replace the dole and unemployment with a new kind of wage for new kinds of work. The equivalent of the dole (or more than the dole) should in the future be paid in a positive way, not as compensation for failure but as an opportunity to achieve. The new kind of wage could be paid as a training subsidy to improve the capacity for future work, or in return for community service not yet adequately performed in our society. This community service would have the advantage of being outside the restrictive jurisdiction of the trade union movement.

Community work such as reading to the blind or to young children in the familiar environments of their own homes; attending to the housekeeping and gardening needs of the disabled or the elderly to enable them to remain in cheaper and more personalised domiciliary (as opposed to institutionalised) care; planting and caring for trees and flowers in public parks, and in many other ways helping to conserve and beautify our natural environment; keeping latch-key children off the streets and enriching their lives. These kinds of activities have often been performed on a voluntary basis by people outside the workforce or people contributing without pay in the time not spent at their formal employment.

What has been done voluntarily and without payment in the past could more often in the future be performed on a paid basis. This would provide more work opportunities for the otherwise unemployed and, by facilitating the domiciliary care of the elderly and of the young, would decrease the cost to the public purse of the burgeoning demands for institutionalised care.

There are those who believe that the only 'true' work involves conventional qualifications. However this ignores the fact that the changing pattern of economic growth will provide fewer jobs in conventional industries. The kinds of jobs that involve caring for others or helping them to discover their creativity should not be perceived as second-best nor as under-using skills. Their development is rather a realistic response to the growing social requirements and productive employment opportunities of the future.

Any major change in our perception of work naturally demands enormous imagination and determination. But far more time, energy and money have been spent on planning and implementing projects which are not nearly so fundamental to the fabric of our society as the personal worth and dignity of so many of its members.

This kind of community service, so strongly advocated by the Australian Churches and by the Australian Democrats, could do much to rebuild the waning sense of community in Australian life. It could do much to help counteract the socially fragmenting effects of the rapidly expanding 'box' industry.

Too many Australians spend their lives moving from one kind of insulated box to another; from the office or factory in a little box on wheels to a larger box on a quarter-acre block to watch the smallest box of them all. More and more Australians are in danger of having little communication with their wider society about anything, except functional matters at their place of paid employment.

There are other options to be considered in an employ-ment policy for the unemployed. One of the most obvious options is to increase the flexibility not only of wage rates but also of work patterns, so that those who would prefer to work part-time rather than full-time are given every opportunity

> ‘If the Hawke Government is serious about wishing to maximise both social justice and economic growth, it needs to preserve the work ethic, with its focus on productivity and reward for effort. But it needs to expand the relevance of this ethic to the community as a whole by encouraging it to apply to socially as well as economically productive employment.’

and encouragement to do so. without its involving an additional on-cost burden for the employer. Given the increasing number of households without dependent children, or with two incomes, this part-time option is one that growing numbers of Australians at different stages of their working lives would like to be able to choose. Of course, *enforced* part-time work or job-sharing would be strongly resented by the trade union movement and by those already sorely pressed trying to rear dependent children in a household with the equivalent of only one average income.

However great the opposition of the trade union movement, there is an urgent need for the Government to lead a comprehensive public debate about new patterns and concepts of work. If this debate does not occur, and instead the dole continues to be paid to one in four young Australians as well as to many pre-retirement-age older Australians, it will not be politically feasible for any Government to go on treating paid employment as if it is the only kind of worthwhile activity. It will be necessary to give more social status to leisure.

This would be easier to do if we were moving more rapidly than we are towards the world depicted by Barry Jones, where the familiar contrast between work and leisure is submerged in a new and wider concept of 'activity', in circumstances where 'work' has been abolished for all but a minority.[21] Nonetheless, if there is an acceleration of the current trend towards shorter and shorter working hours, it may not be too long before work is perceived as the new leisure activity.

In such circumstances, education will be the greatest leisure industry. It will be especially significant in the likely paradoxical situation where the majority who know least about how to use their leisure have too much of it; while the minority who know most about it have no leisure at all. The real beneficiaries of education for leisure will be those most accustomed to being programmed by others and therefore least able to exercise personal initiative in using their own time creatively and constructively for their own personal satisfaction. What they most need for quality leisure is education that helps them develop a personal core: a personal 'cud' to chew.

The prospect of increased leisure is one of the many new problems that should be faced in the educational revolution this country so obviously requires. Too much of the recent education debate has suggested that all that matters about education is how much money governments should be prepared to spend on it, to which educational institutions it should go and in which quantities. This has led to far too little attention being paid to important qualitative questions like the purposes of education and the environments and techniques most suited to achieving them. While politicians are too often as reluctant to discuss the purposes of education as they are to discuss the purposes of society, education is certainly about far more than the protection of a dual government and non-government system through the provision of adequate funds.

Because there is no community consensus about *what* values should be promoted in education, there can be no

> 'One of the most obvious options is to increase the flexibility of work patterns, so that those who would prefer to work part-time rather than full-time are given every opportunity and encouragement to do so.'

acceptable single system. Some think education should promote social change; others think it should protect the status quo. Some think education should promote a specific religion; others think it should teach a spirit of inquiry about *all* religions. Some think education should train people for jobs; others think it should prepare people for the absence of jobs. Some think education should develop people as individuals in their own right; others think education should concentrate on developing people who can fit into the wider society.

My own view is that the primary purpose of education is to help people develop a sense of personal competence and, with it, a crucial sense of self-worth. This provides a special challenge for educators in an era when we have not been able to rely on Governments providing adequate opportunities for competence and worth to be confirmed by conventional paid employment. Because the development of a sense of personal competence begins in early childhood, it is important to reverse the current status hierarchy in our education system, where the greatest professional recognition and financial rewards are given to university educators, rather than to those charged with the vital task of identifying, with sensitivity and skill, the talents and handicaps of the very young.

This is not necessarily best done in the setting of the average modern school, which is often artificially removed from the wider community environment to which the student is trying to relate. But while many schools are isolated from that environment, they are expected to compensate for its limitations. Many of the complaints against our education system are in fact complaints about the negative aspects of our changing society. Schools are increasingly called upon to fill the vacuum that used to be filled by close-knit communication within family and local community life. Now educators are being asked to be social welfare workers as well. They are being constantly pressured to extend the boundaries of the conventional education system to moderate our social problems, or to prevent them from occurring in the first place.

The education system is now expected to compensate for any negative effects arising from women's voluntary or enforced entry into the workforce. Schools are now being expected to give the kind of caring encouragement that used to be provided by that very fine educator, the mother-educator who offered discipline and warmth in that irreplaceable kind of combination that is an

> ‘Schools are increasingly called upon to fill the vacuum that used to be filled by close-knit communication within family and local community life.’

essential part of educating the young to feel competent and worthwhile. Nowadays, many mothers – like many fathers – have insufficient time to spend on their educative role inside the home, because they choose or are obliged to spend so much of their time and energy in paid work outside the home.

In the absence of the former family support system, and given the over-use in most Australian homes of that chewing gum for the eyes, television, the modern education system has a lot of extra work to do that used to be effectively done in the home. Whether today's educational institutions can meet this challenge is another question. What is obvious is that education is being currently used as the scapegoat for some of the more negative aspects of rapid change in our society.

Education is certainly being made the scapegoat for unemployment. Is the basic problem that people don't want to employ the young because they are, by definition, inexperienced? Or is it rather that potential employers don't like what the young have been taught? While there's a lot of talk about the need to return to the 3Rs, we need to add to education another 2Rs and a C. The C is for computer literacy, to discourage the perpetuation of an untenable division between two separate cultures: the technological and the humanist. The other 2Rs we need to add to our education system stand for reasoning and research. For an emphasis on criticial inquiry is essential to Australia's capacity for innovation and flexible response.

In an environment of intense economic competition and rapid social change, educators should concentrate on teaching people how to ask the most pertinent questions, instead of merely imparting information which is often irrelevant by the time the student is in a position to put it to practical use.

The best kind of education is summed up in the reply I received from a seasoned adviser to many Italian Prime Ministers in response to my complaint that he had given only a half-answer to my question: 'It was not a half-answer to your question. It was an answer to your question. If you want better answers, ask better questions.'

Education for an increasingly competitive world involves the capacity to define tomorrow's problems and opportunities today. But modern education requires something else as well to counteract the tendency for more and more of the best quality minds to be confined to more and more specialised areas, working in depth but not also with breadth. The more technically complex the problems of rapid change and the more specialist the skills required to cope with it, the greater the need for many of our best quality minds to be trained in analytical capacities often associated with a generalist education. I have in mind the talent for lateral and integrative thinking; the interest in the broad overview which can see connections between factors previously regarded as unconnected; and the inclination to relate parts of a problem to the whole, assisting a more creative approach or solution.

One of the major challenges for today's educators is to help to avert the threatened polarisation between a relatively small elite able to move with advancing technologies, and a much larger proportion of people whose skills have become outmoded and who lack the right kind of education and the appropriate mental attitudes to be able to adapt to change. Such polarisation could form the basis of yet another class war in Australia: between, on the one hand, that part of labour and capital belonging to the new techintelligentsia, and, on the other, the irrelevant discards. The whole focus of our education system should be on helping to ensure that as many Australians as possible are the beneficiaries rather than the victims of change.

This requires us to get rid of the attitude to education that is part of the broader attitude we have in this country of stressing the development of our natural, but not of our human, resources. If we really cared about our human resources, we would replace the dole not only with new concepts of community work but also with positive educational subsidies. These would either help people train for specific kinds of jobs likely to exist in the future, or equip them for greater leisure – preferably both. If we were really worried about our human resources, we wouldn't allow people to leave school early, merely to join the lost generation of young unemployed. In Australia we have what should be regarded as an intolerably high rate of early departure from schools. Whereas at the age of seventeen years, more than 90 per cent of Japanese are still at school and more than 80 per cent in the United States, in Australia we can barely muster

40 per cent. OECD figures show that Australian retention levels in education are among the lowest in the Western world.

If we want to help solve our current unemployment problem, we need to encourage more of our youth to stay on at school in a creative and positive way: not as alleged preparation for jobs many young people never get, but to benefit from a combination of formal education in the schools concurrent with practical experience in the work place outside. The school system might itself be responsible for providing the outside work, in co-operation with industry and local communities able to identify opportunities for students to perform economically and socially useful tasks. Policy-makers certainly should do more to promote the spread of concurrent education, where formal education and practical work-experience go hand in hand. They also need to promote the concept of recurrent education as something to be experienced many times throughout a lifetime as an essential part of remaining employed in the same or in new kinds of work. The concept of recurrent education is quite different from the widespread community notion of education as a one-off experience that happens at only one stage of a person's life – at a young age, rather than in middle or old age.

While education has typically been discussed in Australia in terms of work, increasingly it will need to be discussed in terms of leisure as well. While it is not yet true that work is the new leisure activity, there will certainly be more emphasis than in the past on the need to use increasing quantities of leisure time as imaginatively as possible. If education is meant to be also for leisure, to what extent will this conflict with education for jobs? Not at all, if you argue that the essence of the best kind of education is to develop the kinds of techniques that create active learners as opposed to the passive taught. The challenge for Australian educators is to motivate people to want to learn. The greatest educators are the self-educators.

This raises the fundamental question of whether our education techniques are geared too much to teaching and not enough to learning. As with Australian industry, so with Australian education, too many structures and processes have been determined by the vested interests and personal convenience of those in control of the system. Like industry patterns and attitudes in this country, and like our attitudes to taxation and social security, education has been geared to precedent rather than to innovation, and to yesterday's world rather than tomorrow's.

The political revolution that has not yet occurred is for Australians to be dragged – by the scruff of their necks if necessary – into the unfamiliar arena of new questions and difficult answers. Without constructive ideas, and the political will to implement them, there is little hope of protecting or promoting an attractive long-term future for this country.

4

We are now moving into a new era in Australian politics when creative ideas and rational policy-making will matter more than ever before. For our major national problem is no longer merely the *political* one of how to redistribute community wealth. We also have the new *economic* problem of how to create wealth in the first place, while accommodating the need for greater security and stability in our changing social environment.

The great danger for Labor's security in government is that it will be more susceptible than non-Labor to union pressures to retard the essential process of wealth creation by a premature and excessive emphasis on wealth redistribution. In this context, it is important to recognise that the Prices and Incomes Accord is less about wage restraint than about the drive for greater union power in the management decisions of companies and Labor Governments. Whether unions are allowed to achieve this power, and how they choose to exercise it, is the most significant single variable in Australia's economic future. Not that the Opposition has managed to convey this basic political fact. It has been too busy talking on the Government's ground rather than its own.

The critical question for the future of the Labor Government is whether it will be able to keep in some rational balance the often conflicting emphases on wealth creation and wealth redistribution. It is obviously easier to do this if taxation, wages and welfare are considered not separately but as part of an integrated policy package, aimed at maximising the potential for wealth creation and minimising the irrationality of wealth distribution. This is the most urgent of the many major policy reforms required to prevent this country from falling further and further behind in an increasingly competitive international race.

The more serious the problem of wealth creation, the less extravagant the pressures are likely to be for wealth redistribution. If Bob Hawke wants to discourage future pressures for extravagant redistribution of wealth, he should emphasise the difficulties involved in wealth creation. While he undoubtedly has a short-term

> ‘It is important to recognise that the Prices and Incomes Accord is less about wage restraint than about the drive for greater union power in the management decisions of companies and Labor Governments.’

interest in electoral rhetoric about national economic recovery, he needs to temper it carefully with an eye to curbing demands for unrealistic wealth redistribution from within the union movement and his own party. The Prime Minister might remember the fate of Malcolm Fraser, whose boom talk helped him scrape home in 1980 but encouraged the economic problems that preceded his electoral defeat in 1983.

Somewhat paradoxically, Bob Hawke best protects the stability of his own Labor Government by supporting the business community's argument about the fragility of economic growth. At the same time, he needs to reassure his party and the trade union faithful that he has not forgotten the social purpose of growth. Profits may be an end in themselves for companies, but not for Labor Leaders who want to avoid internal party revolution. Bob Hawke's future as Leader and Prime Minister depends on his capacity to reassure his Labor followers that, however slowly, he is nonetheless marching in the ideologically correct direction towards a more equitable society. Hence his extreme sensitivity to criticism that his Government's second Budget gave too much to those already well-off.

Gradual change is the key to the continued success of the Hawke Government. If it is forced to agree to demands for wealth redistribution that exceed what is reasonable in view of the pace of wealth creation, it will be removed from office.

Excessive redistribution of wealth is not the only issue on which a non-Labor revival might occur. For politics is about more than the financial values registered in our standard of living. It is also about the essentially non-financial values relating to the need for greater security and stability in our social environment. Increasing numbers of marginal voters fear their material well-being may be very short-lived, because of the social instability around them into which they fear they may inevitably be drawn. More and more haves fear they might soon fall into the ranks of the havenots through their failure or their children's failure to find work, or through the breakdown of their marriages, or through a combination of both.

It can no longer be assumed, as it used to be in the Menzies era, that material well-being is the basis of social stability. The reverse is now perceived to be the case. This is one of the major revolutions in Australian politics that the Opposition failed to exploit. It will doubtless be a basic theme in the new conservatism following the next national election, when politicians may eventually catch up with the electorate's view that, without social stability, there will be no economic security; without stabilising employment policies and a restored sense of family responsibility, there will be no 'Utopia Unlimited', to use Sir Henry Bolte's phrase.

The new conservatives will not be small l Liberals, who have had their day in Australian politics. In the past, Labor has gained enormously from small l Liberalism, which acted as the vital bridge without which voters would have found it much more difficult than they did to cross over from supporting conservative Liberals like Sir Robert Menzies and Malcolm Fraser to supporting Labor Leaders like Gough Whitlam and Bob Hawke.

> 'It can no longer be assumed, as it used to be in the Menzies era, that material well-being is the basis of social stability. The reverse is now perceived to be the case. This is one of the major revolutions in Australian politics that the Opposition failed to exploit.'

Nowadays, this bridging role is no longer relevant, for some of the perspectives of the small l Liberals are to the left rather than the right of the Hawke Labor Government. The same party labels have assumed a different political meaning, and small l Liberals are now on some issues closer to Labor's Centre-Left and Socialist Left factions than to Labor's right wing. This is not to suggest that the small l Liberals could easily form an effective political alliance with the Socialist Left, except on such attitudes as radical feminism with its accompanying emphasis on the socialised care of children from a so-called 'community' base rather than a more strongly supported family base.

Labor, of course, has a vested electoral interest in encouraging the small l Liberal view that the future of the non-Labor parties lies in the small l Liberal territory that part of the Labor spectrum is already occupying so effectively. So long as the non-Labor parties can be persuaded to believe that their future does not lie in moving further to the right, Labor can respond to its political opposition with minimum strains on its own internal unity.

It is easy for the Labor Government to accommodate both the left and the centre of the Australian political spectrum without incurring the ideological hostility of the more radical party members who at the moment constitute the most rapidly expanding section of the ALP's rank and file.

The real strains on Labor unity would occur if Labor were forced much further to the right by a coherently conservative political opposition, which pitched its appeal to the two groups I have always regarded as electorally decisive in Australian politics: the peasant conservatives on their suburban quarter-acre blocks, and the downwardly-mobile but essentially conservative genteel poor, who have fallen on hard times but never like to talk about it. More and more of the peasant conservatives are now in fear of joining the ranks of the genteel poor. These are the two groups who make or break Governments. These are also the two groups who would most eagerly respond to a new conservative movement based on imaginative employment policies, combined with a strong commitment to the restoration of social cohesion and a proper sense of family responsibility.

This kind of humane conservatism has not yet surfaced in non-Labor politics, but had it appeared under Andrew Peacock's leadership, it could have done much to consolidate conservative support across conventional party lines. Based on the social values still dominant in Australian marginal seats, it could have provided a clear and favourable contrast with the exclusively economic and corporatist emphasis of the Hawke Labor Government.

But as things turned out, the Opposition failed to fight on the *social* ground where the Government's record was weakest. Instead, as if they had a political death-wish, the Opposition parties chose to fight on the *economic* ground where the Government's record was strongest. Inevitably, the non-Labor parties were seen to be beaten at the old growth game they used to play so well.

Displaced from their old political ground, the non-Labor parties have failed to fight as they needed to do on new political ground of their own choosing. Fractured by irreconcilable divisions between small l Liberals and conservatives, the Liberal and National Parties were unable to agree within their own ranks about the rules of the new social unity game they might have played with some electoral credibility. Lacking the necessary inspirational captain with firm intellectual convictions and real fire in his belly, the Opposition also lacked a cohesive political team. They had no fight in them, and just stood idly by as Labor captured their ground and then, unchallenged, proceeded to redefine the political game on Labor's terms.

> **'The Opposition failed to fight on the *social* ground where the Government's record was weakest. Instead, as if they had a political death-wish, the Opposition parties chose to fight on the *economic* ground where the Government's record was strongest.'**

The non-Labor parties are still in a state of political shock, too stunned to think strategically about how best they might re-position themselves to encourage a political comeback. So far, they have been content to mouth conventional responses about Labor's propensity to self-destruct. The Hawke Government, the Opposition says, will destroy itself by acceding to excessive union demands for greater power over national economic strategy. Or it will be destroyed by the continuing influx of Socialist Left rank-and-file members; or by the fracturing of the Prime Minister's original power base in the NSW Right; or by too much of the mud sticking from Andrew Peacock's September 1984 allegations that the Hawke Government wound up the Costigan Royal Commission when correspondence apparently showed it to be within an ace of identifying financiers of organised crime.

Some or all of these factors may turn out to be extremely relevant to Labor's political future. But waiting for opponents to destroy themselves is hardly the way to build non-Labor strength, or respect for the non-Labor cause, in Australian politics. Something much more constructive is required. The Opposition needs to commit itself to a revolutionary new approach to policy-making in this country. And the Liberal partner in the non-Labor coalition needs to commit itself to a revolutionary new approach to party management.

Despite the Liberals' claim to represent the interests and needs of the business sector, they are prepared to accept in their own organisation standards of performance that would not be tolerated in any competent company. In the business world, if the community is obviously not wanting to invest in a company or buy its product, the management is sacked or the company wound up. In the Liberal Party, while ineffectual parliamentary leaders are eventually replaced, the organisational leaders – both the amateurs and the paid support staff remain entrenched. This is as unprofessional for a political party as it is for any business which genuinely wants to beat its competitors. Tomorrow's successful strategies will never emerge from those who presided over yesterday's failures.

This kind of truism has always fallen on deaf Liberal ears, notoriously reluctant to listen to what they don't want to hear. Instead, the reaction to the party's poor performance has been to appoint unthreatening committees of inquiry, comprising not objective outside critics but the kinds of party members who can be relied upon to discuss the symptoms and not the basic causes of the Liberals being chained to opposition.

> *'Despite the Liberals' claim to represent the interests and needs of the business sector, they are prepared to accept in their own organisation standards of performance that would not be tolerated in any competent company.'*

Of course, there is no need for a committee of inquiry to discover the widely-held view that unless the Liberal Party is prepared to throw off its albatross of dead wood and replenish its ranks with people of intellectual calibre and persuasive skills, it runs the risk of being edged out by a more effective non-Labor force.

Many Liberals, however, do not share this perspective. They argue that a firm non-Labor base already exists in New South Wales where John Howard is among a nucleus of competent Federal parliamentarians and where, at the State level, the Liberals under Nick Greiner are mounting an effective challenge to the Wran Labor Government.

Among those who are more critical of Liberal performance, many put their faith not in the New South Wales Liberal Party but in the electorally successful Queensland National Party, which they claim would provide a much firmer organisational base for expanding non-Labor strength in national politics.

The link between Liberal and National Parties might be strengthened, some argue, by the close personal association between Sir Robert Sparkes, President of the Queensland National Party, and Malcolm Fraser, former Liberal Prime Minister from Victoria. Others maintain that the most effective link between the two non-Labor parties might in the immediate future be provided by Paul Everingham, currently representing the Country Liberal Party as Chief Minister of the Northern Territory but hoping to enter national politics at the next election. Straddling both Liberal and National Parties, Paul Everingham is outside the traditional rivalries in non-Labor politics between small and big l Liberals and between New South Wales and Victorian Liberal machines.

There is a strong case for arguing that the potentially most effective momentum for the revival of non-Labor politics would come from neither the Liberal nor the National Party but rather from a new conservative movement led by people not yet in the national parliament, and therefore not tarnished by negative aspects of past non-Labor performance.

It was obvious at the time of Malcolm Fraser's near-defeat in 1980 that non-Labor politics urgently required a fresh start – a clear break with the past. They needed a populist revival of the kind Robert Menzies led in the mid 1940s, when the new Liberal Party replaced the decimated United Australia Party. But to the emotional enthusiasm of the 1940's movement, the non-Labor movement of the 1980s would have needed to add intellectual conviction and tough argument against the 'consensus' claims of the Hawke

Government. The 1980's populist revival has never occurred. It should have been provided by Andrew Peacock on taking over as Liberal Leader in 1983. But he failed to exploit the opportunity, unduly influenced by the high level of Bob Hawke's personal popularity.

To compete with Labor, any future non-Labor revival must be based on quality candidates and quality ideas. The current crisis of non-Labor politics is the notable shortage of each of these vital ingredients in an era when Labor is better endowed with both of them than ever before. Enormously dependent on the intellectual calibre of his own front bench, Bob Hawke has had good reason to quote the words of his mentor John Curtin that 'it is thinking which is the great auxiliary of this [Labor] Party'. Without his high-quality Ministry, Bob Hawke would doubtless have faced the kinds of problems that bedevilled the Whitlam era when Ministerial talent was in much shorter supply.

'There is a strong case for arguing that the potentially most effective momentum for the revival of non-Labor politics would come from neither the Liberal nor the National Party but rather from a new conservative movement led by people not yet in the national parliament, and therefore not tarnished by negative aspects of past non-Labor performance.'

But regardless of the dramatic improvement in the calibre of Labor Ministries, it still remains true that the level of debate between the parties in Australian politics is far too low, given the complexity and urgency of our national problems. There is no sign of the sinewy, intellectually powerful debate that in the United States commands electoral respect. It is difficult enough to have policy issues discussed in terms of technicalities, more difficult still to have them discussed in terms of future trends, but almost impossible to have them discussed in terms of social values and ethical judgements.

The Opposition has merely followed the lead of the Labor Government in pursuing a kind of Marxist reductionism that systematically views all national problems in economic and not social terms. This often leads politicians to treat the economic symptoms of national problems rather than their non-economic cause. This is a costly way of ensuring that the problems remain.

But even when unambiguously economic questions are being discussed, there is a general tendency in Australian politics to do so in generalised terminology which obscures the value judgements that need to be debated.

Take the example of 'profit', which has such a vital bearing on economic growth and on the formulation of a national tax policy which would balance what Bob Hawke describes as the twin aims of 'efficiency' and 'equity'. Obviously the term 'profit' needs to be further refined to draw a whole range of distinctions between different kinds of profit. Distinctions need to be drawn between profit received by companies and by individuals[22], in terms of scale and economic implications. In an era when economic growth is increasingly capital-intensive – involving very much higher levels of investment and profit than those to which Australians have in the past been accustomed – profit needs to be discussed not only in terms of its absolute size but also in terms of the level of investment and degree of risk required to gain it.[23]

In our newly deregulated environment, distinctions need to

be drawn between profit which is removed from our use and profit which is ploughed back into the Australian economy through further company investment or recycling of company taxation. Distinctions also need to be drawn between the different origins of profit. Should there be tax incentives for 'productive' investment and disincentives against 'speculative' investment? If so, how should those categories be defined? Is it 'productive' to encourage Australians to sink such a large proportion of national savings in the family home and quarter-acre block? Can the unnatural profits from protected industry be said to be obtained from 'productive' investment if they are used to replace people by machines?

The value judgements involved in such questions should be the substance of public debate. Yet they seldom are. Our political system seems unable or unprepared to define for itself and the community exactly what are, and what are not, legitimate demands on the taxpayer and the taxgatherer.

For most of the post-war period, non-Labor Governments have not had to face up to the politics of priorities and redistribution, since they have typically seen themselves as not merely born to rule but also born to an environment of economic growth. Now, given the raised welfare expectations of the Whitlam era and the increased welfare demands being currently caused by unemployment and family breakdown, many are questioning the capacity of our social and economic structures to withstand the strain.

In the late 'sixties, there were almost four taxpayers to every one person on welfare; a decade later, the number of taxpayers per person on welfare had almost halved to only 2.5.

We are in immediate danger of collapsing under the weight of a social welfare system geared to treating the economic symptoms, but not the basic policy and attitudinal causes, of the social instability which is crippling this country. Money will alleviate the suffering, but do nothing to cure the problem. Unless politicians are prepared to address the social causes of rising welfare demands, there is no way of arresting the drift towards two antagonistic societies: one of them based on the Puritan work ethic and the other on its absence. In one society, a sense of direction, prestige and identity can be gained by occupational achievement; in the other society it is often hard for those on welfare benefits to establish any sense of personal worth at all.

The result has been the growth of a new counter-culture in Australia, reflecting not the peace-loving 'flower-power' of the 'sixties but instead a frightening kind of social aggression. There are already disturbingly clear signs of the vulnerability of the counter-culture to gang warfare and exploitation by organised crime. In the absence of socially productive employment to replace the dole, the values of violence all too easily replace the values of conventional work. Participants in the work ethic culture have reason to fear the new counter-culture, not merely because the cost of supporting it threatens their capacity to support their own families but also because the contrasting values of peaceful work and of aggressive idleness cannot viably co-exist within the one community. Yet however different the cultures, they can't be segregated by some kind of geographical apartheid.

If politicians want to avoid the drift towards a dangerously polarised community, they must address the social implications of the increasingly uneven impact of economic growth on different groups and industries and regions. The Hawke Government needs to acknowledge that if you are unemployed, the relevant unemployment statistic is 100 per cent and not the 9 per cent of the work force that the Minister for Employment, Ralph Willis, cites. The more the Government lauds the economic growth that the unemployed are not personally experiencing, the greater their alienation from the system as a whole. Generalised talk about growth for the 'nation' or the 'community' ignores the fact that for many unemployed individuals there is no growth at all: neither material, nor spiritual.

There is a marked insensitivity in the way the Labor Government views the political world in terms of collective aggregates rather than individuals and families.

Just as insensitive is the way the Opposition has focused on sectional party philosophy. This massages the non-Labor party faithful, but vacates the vital conser-

> 'In a choice between the rhetoric of national patriotism and of sectional party, Australian voters choose patriotism every time.'

vative ground that Sir Robert Menzies firmly held by depicting Liberalism as essentially non-sectional and *Australian*. In a choice between the rhetoric of national patriotism and of sectional party, Australian voters choose patriotism every time. The same is true of a choice between state patriotism and sectional party. This explains why in Victorian state politics the patriot par excellence, Sir Henry Bolte has had far more appeal than the more sectional Liberal Leader, Jeff Kennett.

In Australian post-war politics, the clear winners always have been the most convincing national or state patriots – whatever party they happen to be representing. Bob Hawke knows this only too well. So did South Australia's wily Liberal Premier, Sir Thomas Playford. He had no doubts at all about the winning power of patriotism rather than party. He once told me:

There are 20 per cent who will vote for you through thick and thin. And there are 20 per cent who will *never* vote for you. Winning elections is a matter of ignoring *all* of this 40 per cent and capturing as many as you can of the remaining 60 per cent by talking not party philosophy but state (or national) interest.

Armed with this basic credo plus an electoral gerrymander, Sir Thomas Playford won elections – every one but the last – for twenty-six years.

A preference for patriotism rather than party was not the only thing Sir Thomas Playford and Bob Hawke have had in common. Both have been undoctrinaire, prepared to abandon sectional party ideology in an effort to consolidate their electoral position. In re-reading an analysis I wrote many years ago of the Playford political style, I am struck by the direct parallels with the contemporary Hawke. If appropriate adjustments are made to the text to accommodate the different party affiliations of the two men, my discussion of the non-Labor Leader Playford could equally apply to our current Labor Leader Hawke:

A few of Playford's political methods have been described even by Labor spokesmen as 'socialistic'. Indeed, in the course of his policy speech for the 1950 State Election, Labor Opposition Leader, Mick O'Halloran, pronounced the Premier's policy to have been 'more socialistic than Labor could ever hope to implement even if it were in office'. Though politically tactless, this assertion was probably accurate, for O'Halloran would have found even greater difficulty than Playford in attempting to force through the Legislative Council legislation like that providing for price and rent control and the nationalisation of the Adelaide Electric Supply Company . . .

Such ideological concessions as Playford has made ...
served a dual purpose. As well as either giving or appearing
to give material advantage to a numerically important sector
of the electorate, they also contributed to Playford's political
image as an undoctrinaire non-Labor Leader, prepared to
adopt 'socialistic' methods
to secure non-sectional
ends. Thus, in 1954, the
Premier was able to deny
quite credibly that his Party
was dominated by only one
of a number of interest
groups: 'Our own Organisation is a Liberal organisation,
and we don't stand for any
particular class of the
community ... We are just as
anxious to look after the right
sort of working man as the business man.' ...

> 'The interesting question many Australians are now asking is whether Bob Hawke, who talks like a Conservative, thinks like a Radical.'

Indeed, this arch-tactician's primary and constant preoccupation with keeping himself in power has meant that his
attitude to the South Australian aristocracy has resembled
Bismarck's to the Junkers. Although anxious to preserve a
conservative society, Playford has rejected those conservative prejudices that threatened his political power. On rare
but nonetheless significant occasions, the Leader of the LCL
has fitted Mrs. Erlynne's description of Lady Jedburgh's
nephew in the second act of *Lady Windermere's Fan:* He
thinks like a Tory, and talks like a Radical, and that's so
important nowadays.[24]

The interesting question many Australians are now asking
is whether Bob Hawke, who talks like a Conservative, thinks

like a Radical. If he is returned to office, will his apparent conservatism last, or will it turn out to have been a technique to gain the confidence of a conservative electorate before leading it gently and gradually in a more radical direction?

If Labor's conservatism turns out to be more than temporary, where does this leave the non-Labor parties? Will they continue to sulk at finding this Labor cuckoo in their nest, or will they begin to react positively by developing a more electorally appealing interpretation of the national interest than Labor's consensus view? Without offending the so-called middle ground of the Australian electorate, will non-Labor move further to the right and force Bob Hawke to do likewise, in the hope that this will split the Labor movement by antagonising the expanding number of radical socialists among its rank-and-file? Or will the non-Labor parties continue instead to make the basic political mistake of being content to compete with Bob Hawke on his own ground and in his own terms?

In the short term at least, the answers to all these questions depend on the Opposition's performance at the coming election. This performance is likely to be improved if Bob Hawke is encouraged to lose control of the campaign by being forced to fight on ground he would not have chosen and therefore could not orchestrate himself.

This ground would include inflammatory and non-consensus issues like the social viability of Australia's immigration programme as discussed by Geoffrey Blainey[25], and the legitimacy of Aboriginal land rights claims. Nor would Bob Hawke welcome accusations of 'consensus' thought control under his Government, or of authoritarian Big Brother prying into pensioners' homes. Nor would he want the Opposition to stress the crippling effect of any EPAC review that legitimised further capital taxes on farmers. Least welcome of all would be any reassertion in the campaign of the allegations made by Andrew Peacock in parliament that the Prime Minister had in some way inhibited an effective attempt to uncover the complex networks of organised crime in this country.

All these issues would be unwelcome to the Prime Minister as threatening the image he likes to project of himself and his Government as being always in rational and calm control of what is important to the Australian community and the national interest. Except for the Combe-Ivanov affair, [26] and later the issue of organised crime, the Prime Minister has been able to play politics on his own ground and according to his own rules. For the Opposition has inexplicably allowed him to be the umpire. If the non-Labor parties manage to break that pattern in the coming election campaign, the vote could be closer than earlier public opinion polls indicated.

'If Labor's conservatism turns out to be more than temporary, where does this leave the non-Labor parties? Will they continue to sulk at finding this Labor cuckoo in their nest, or will they begin to react positively by developing a more electorally appealing interpretation of the national interest than Labor's consensus view?'

Depending on that vote, there are alternative scenarios for non-Labor politics after the next election. If the Opposition polls well in marginal seats, the existing non-Labor party structures could remain unchanged. The Liberal and National Parties could retain their separate identities, ambitions and rivalries, preserving the precarious balance of tensions between them that I have always described as a varying state of civil and uncivil war.

But the political effectiveness of the old non-Labor structures would still depend, as it has always done, on the quality of leadership. 'Follow the Leader' may be a well-known children's game, but it is also the central assumption on which non-Labor politics have always been based. A non-Labor party relies on its Leader not only as the focus of its appeal to the electorate but also as the fount of party policy. The quality of that policy depends all too much on the Leader's intellectual creativity and on his or her inclination and capacity to impose the stamp of personal political authority.

Policy-making problems are not helped by the ludicrous situation in Liberal politics where if followers advocate basic policy changes, they are often accused of being disloyal to the Leader. Intellectual creativity and party loyalty should not be juxtaposed in this way. Yet because they are, the result has been the kind of policy immobilism that led me to suggest in my 1980 Alfred Deakin Lecture that the two mottos for the contemporary Liberal Party should be:

DON'T JUST DO SOMETHING; STAND THERE!

and

THE FUTURE IS THE PRESENT RENOVATED.

If its marked lack of policy creativity encourages a poor result for the Opposition in marginal seats, this would provide an additional impetus to existing pressures for a new political movement with new people and new ideas. As well as attracting fresh talent into national politics, such a movement could presumably gather in some existing Liberal and National Party parliamentarians. It could also provide an extra option for concerned and/or personally ambitious business executives disillusioned with what they perceive to be the electoral ineffectiveness of current non-Labor appeals. Of course, reservations are widely held about the electoral danger of allowing any populist non-Labor revival to be converted into a sectional business operation, in which social issues are considered to be merely residual to a basic economic emphasis. Also many people would have very reasonable qualms about the way in which company executives could be prone to view a political movement as something to be taken over with the ruthlessness they have shown in swallowing up rival companies.

> '‘Follow the Leader’ may be a well-known children's game, but it is also the central assumption on which non-Labor politics have always been based.'

Any new political movement that wanted to establish itself with the electorate would need to have very positive and creative views on how best to promote the kind of economic growth that combines national wealth creation with individual opportunity for the currently deprived. This kind of humane politics would be an amalgam of what is best in each of the three major political movements in our country.

It would draw on the social cohesion emphasis of conservatism, on the social justice concerns of socialism, and on the commitment of liberalism to trying to ensure adequate opportunity to every individual to fulfil his or her potential with maximum freedom of personal choice, tempered by a sense of social responsibility.

The consensus rhetoric of the early days of the Hawke Government promised all this, but failed to deliver. With its conservative emphasis on the need for national economic growth, but its lack of concern for social cohesion, for social justice and for individual expression, the Hawke revolution seems to have stopped halfway.

Endnotes

1. Address to the Autumn Seminar of the Australian Institute of Public Administration (ACT Group), 28 March 1983, published as 'Corporatism in Australia – The Case of the National Economic Summit' in *Canberra Bulletin of Public Administration*, vol. X no. 3 (Spring 1983), pp. 9 – 12.

2. Address to the Australian Institute of Mining and Metallurgy, published in *The Australian*, 6 August 1984.

3. *Weekend Australian*, 28 – 29 July 1984, p. 7.

4. Television interview with Robert Haupt and Trevor Kennedy, *Sunday*, Channel 9, 5 August 1984.

5. *Australian Liberalism and the Need For Change*, The Alfred Deakin Lecture Trust, Melbourne, September 1980.

6. A survey of large mining and manufacturing companies by the Business Council of Australia revealed that in 1983 direct wages grew by 3.3% but on-costs by 14.4%.

7. *The Liberal Approach to Change*, The Alfred Deakin Lecture Trust, Melbourne, July 1983.

8. *Facing the Facts: Report of the Liberal Party Committee of Review*, Liberal Party of Australia, Canberra, September 1983.

9. There is a detailed discussion of these pressures in Paul Kelly, *The Hawke Ascendancy*, Angus & Robertson, Sydney 1984.

10. This has been underlined by the defection from the ALP to the Nuclear Disarmament Party of former Victorian Senator Jean Melzer.

11. Address to the State Council of the Victorian Liberal Party, 21 July 1984.

12. 'An open letter to Hawke on behalf of Australia's poor', *The Age*, 28 July 1984, p. 19.

13. *ibid*.

14. Quoted in *The Weekend Australian*, 11 – 12 August 1984, Magazine p. 16.

15. 'Future Economic and Social Environments' in *National Leisure Seminar: Discussion Papers*, Victorian Government Printer, Melbourne 1983, p. 115.

16. The instability of plural societies is discussed in greater detail in Katharine West, 'Stratification and Ethnicity in "Plural" New States', *Race*, The Institute of Race Relations, London, vol. XIII, no. 4, 1972, pp. 487 – 495.

17. *Australian Liberalism and the Need For Change, op. cit.*, p. 5.

18. Katharine West 'Federalism and Resources Development: The Politics of State Inequality', in Allan Patience and Jeffrey Scott (eds), *Australian Federalism: Future Tense*, Oxford University Press, Melbourne 1983, pp. 107 – 122.

19. Sir Arvi Parbo, 'The Minerals Industry in July 1984', Melbourne address, 27 July 1984.

20. Barry Jones, 'Future Work and Leisure Environment' in *National Leisure Seminar: Discussion Papers, op. cit.*, p. 132.

21. Katharine West, 'Issues for Discussion: An Overview of the Seminar Papers', *ibid*.

22. The lack of agreement in Australian society about the right to profit from private ownership is discussed in Katharine West, 'The Politics of Greenspace', *Greenspace in the Cities*, Australian Institute of Urban Studies, Canberra 1977, pp. 56 – 63.

23. Community attitudes to profit in the mining industry are discussed in Katharine West, 'Mineral Development: Political Realities', *Minerals and Australia in the World to the Year 2000*, Australian Mining Industry Council, Canberra 1982, pp. 15 – 22.

24. Katharine West, *Power in the Liberal Party*, Cheshire, Melbourne 1965, pp. 58 – 59.

25. Geoffrey Blainey's controversial public comments were later succinctly outlined in *All for Australia*, Methuen Haynes, Sydney 1984.

26. This has been discussed in detail by David Marr in *The Ivanov Trail*, Nelson, Melbourne 1984.